For information about permission to reproduce selections of this book, write to Ulrike Wiethaus, Department of Religion, Wake Forest University, PO Box 7212, Winston Salem, NC 29109

First Edition 2012

ISBN-13: 978-1469949567
ISBN-10: 1469949563

Designed by CreateSpace and Ulrike Wiethaus

Ray Littleturtle, Lumbee Traditionalist, Robeson County, North Carolina (d. January 10, 2011)

The Brothers of the Buffalo would like to thank and present this book as a dedication to Ray Littleturtle, without whom this project would not have been possible. Now you are free with the great ones.
AHO

Brothers of the Buffalo Speak Up

Contemporary American Indian Prison Writings

EDITED BY BROTHERS OF THE BUFFALO PRAYER CIRCLE AND ULRIKE WIETHAUS

2012

Through autobiography, art, and poetry, this book brings together American Indian prison writings to rethink stereotypes and to imagine new ways of culturally based justice for American Indian men, women, and their families.

CONTENTS

ACKNOWLEDGEMENTS

Many people assisted in the creation of this project and supported the Brothers of the Buffalo circle. Most of all, we thank the following Elders for their counsel, prayers, and faith in the circle: Tom Belt (ᎠᏂᎩᏍᏩᎩ, United Keetoowah Band of Cherokee Indians), Naca Harry Charger (Lakota), Chief Leon Locklear (Tuscarora, NC), Chief Alberto W. Lorenzo (Triqui Nation, Oaxaca), and Wendsler Nosie (San Carlos Apache). A very special thank you to Chief Leon's family and Michael Jacobs (Cherokee) for bringing the gift of traditional songs, drumming, and contemporary music to AXCI. At Alexander Correctional Institution (AXCI), Chaplain Daniel Redding provided unfaltering support and encouragement. Keith Whitener, Superintendent of the AXCI prison administration, provided leadership and vision. We are grateful to Doug Walker, Assistant Superintendent for Programs and Treatment, for his understanding and flexibility. On behalf of all of us, thank you! At Wake Forest University, many thanks to the students who listened to and shared with the Brothers of the Buffalo, and who contributed individual and team research in collaboration with the Brothers, and to the Religion Department and Divinity School student assistants who transcribed the original chapters. Many thanks to the Divinity School graduate students who assisted with the graphic design of the cover by Snow Hawk, and who supported the project by taking care of administrative details. Thank you also to the Religion and Public Engagement (RPE) initiative and the Department of Religion for understanding the importance of this project, for technical support, and for RPE's funding support for student work.

A special thanks to the Divinity School for encouraging Divinity School graduate students in their work on behalf of the project. A big thank you to the families of the Brothers of the Buffalo prayer circle who supported their relatives and cooked so much good food for the 2010

Green Corn Festival that brought us together before many of the authors were moved to other facilities.

All proceeds of the sale of this publication will be donated to support religious freedom for American Indian inmates and to assist American Indian communities and individuals and their families to prevent incarceration and recidivism. Special thanks go to the Wake Forest University Institute of Public Engagement, the Wake Forest University Community Law and Business Clinic, and the Wake Forest University legal services.

The full page art work, including the cover art, is by members of the Brothers of the Buffalo. Throughout the book, names have often been changed to protect the privacy of the authors and their families. The photo of Ray Littleturtle is courtesy of public domain, http://www.fold3.com/page/283934569_ray_littleturtle_clark/. The photo of Brothers of the Buffalo prayer circle members is courtesy of AXCI's Chaplaincy Office. The image of the eagle is courtesy of Microsoft clip art. The eagle design has been chosen in honor of Raven, an Inuit Elder of the Brothers of the Buffalo.

FOREWORD

I was a new Chaplain in a new facility when American Indians at Alexander Correctional were allowed to build their Prayer Circle. Together, we acquired the rocks for the four directions. We painted the rocks with the proper colors: red, yellow, black and white. At that time, I understood the significance and symbolism of the circle intellectually, but it was not until I saw American Indian practitioners smudge, enter the circle and pray for the first time that I began to understand the meaning of the circle with my heart. With tears in their eyes, tears that expressed a depth of meaning that words cannot convey, American Indian brothers gave thanks to the Creator for their circle. They gave thanks for those who were present and for those who, through the years, would enter the circle. This group of men would soon become the Brothers of the Buffalo prayer circle. Since that time, I have seen the flow of time in the prayer circle. I see the Brothers' relationship with inmates who have come before, the relationship with those who are now here, and with those who will come through in the coming years. Yet I see in the men who enter the prayer circle an even deeper connection. It is a bond with ancient ancestors who have come before the arrival of Europeans, a bond created by the Creator to whom the Brothers direct their prayers.

In the circle, the Brothers become one with each other and with all of creation, where we have our beginning and our final resting place. Here, the Brothers find a kind of peace and direction that is difficult to experience in the correctional setting. As you read these stories, in all their honesty, it is my prayer that you, too, will see connections that enable you to find peace and direction.

Chaplain Daniel Redding
Alexander Correctional Institution

INTRODUCTION: OTHER CIRCLES OF MOTION

Ulrike Wiethaus

"To pray
you open your whole self
To sky, to earth, to sun, to moon
To one whole voice that is you.

And know there is more
That you can't see, can't hear,
Can't know except in moments
Steadily growing, and in languages
That aren't always sound but other
Circles of motion."

Joy Harjo (Muskogee),
Eagle Poem[1]

This collection of essays has been born of efforts, individual and communal, to make visible that which many people don't see and don't know: the lives of American Indian inmates not as stereotyped convicts, but as sons, brothers, husbands, fathers, and kin.[2] For over a year, the Brothers of the Buffalo worked collectively to gather the poetry and write and assemble the essays and art work. Together with Wake Forest University undergraduate and graduate students, we co-designed the cover art and typed the hand-written essays. This introduction provides some background information on the context of this book and its authors. Although the spiritual circle of the Brothers of the Buffalo at Alexander Correctional Institution, Taylorsville, NC, includes members of tribes from across the continent, the majority of the authors' tribal homelands are located across the Carolinas and adjacent regions.[3]For more than twelve thousand years, Native peoples have lived in what is today called North Carolina. Originally numbering over thirty tribes, Indigenous peoples created a diversity of cultural, spiritual, and political systems, and spoke languages rooted in the AlgonquIan, Siouan and IroquoIan linguistic families. Today, Indian communities in North Carolina constitute the seventh largest Indigenous population in the United States, and the most numerous Native community east of the Mississippi. There are currently eight tribes who are state or federally recognized. An additional number of communities are preparing for such recognition. Federally and state recognized tribes in North Carolina include the Coharie, the Eastern Band of Cherokee, the Haliwa Saponi, the Lumbee, the Meherrin, the Occaneechi Band of Saponi Nation, the Sappony, and the Waccamaw-Siouan tribe. Alexander Correctional Institution (AXCI) began as a maximum security prison, which is the oldest form of correctional institutions; "maximum security" means that prisoners are monitored continuously via video cameras and prison guards, and that security measures in the form of secured gate and wall systems are at their highest. Rather than modern institutions such as AXCI, American Indian and Indigenous prison stereotypes often evoke Hollywood films about the "Wild West" and images of imprisoned Indian leaders such as Goyaałé (Geronimo, 1829-1909), Tȟatȟáŋka Íyotake (Sitting Bull, c. 1831-1890) and Tȟašúŋke Witkó (Crazy Horse, 1840-1877).[4] Indeed, prisons have played a central part in the history of US-Native relations. The imprisonment of more than a thousand Dakota men after the US-Dakota War of 1862 led to the largest mass execution of prisoners on American soil. The 1969-1971 occupation of Alcatraz Island by the American Indian Movement (AIM) is as known internationally as is the case of Leonard Peltier (Anishinabe and Dakota/Lakota, b. 1944), both trenchant examples of encounters between federal law and Indigenous activism.[5] For the more than five hundred tribes in the United States today, even the current difficult legal status of Indian reservations can still be experienced as a form of imprisonment, and as the life story of Sitting Bull demonstrates so forcefully, it had been intentionally designed to be so in its early phase of implementation.[6] American Indian scholars point out that in the pre-contact era, prisons did not exist on Turtle Island. Native nations had culturally appropriate, functioning judicial systems in place. These included a spiritual dimension and focused on restitution rather than retribution.[7] With the imposition of Western penal systems, the loss and diminishment of Indian sovereignty also has meant the loss and diminishment of Indigenous nations' self-determination in shaping jurisdiction for its members. Today, American Indian men and women have to work within a Euro-American legal system on the state and federal level that has historically been slow to recognize and acknowledge the uniqueness and value of Indigenous justice traditions. Yet there have always also been individual and collective American Indian efforts to impact US legal policies on behalf of American Indian communities. For example, Lakota community leader Robert Sundance (1927 - 1993), himself illegally arrested close to 500 times, is highly regarded for his activist work to change arrest and conviction procedures for homeless alcoholics. The Los Angeles non-profit organization United American Indian Involvement has named a family wellness center after him.[8]

For female and male inmates, a Euro-American lack of understanding of American Indian spirituality and diminished Native sovereignty can become a daily issue when working with prison administrators, especially in the area of religious freedom.[9] An experience of a lack of religious freedom may include not receiving culturally appropriate prison ministry, not being allowed to practice ceremonies, or not being permitted to wear long hair. Sweat lodge ceremonies are a particular area of conflict for state prisons. For example, in 2007, the American Civil Liberties Union (ACLU) of Alabama represented Native American inmates in their successful lawsuit requiring the state of Alabama to permit sacred sweat lodge ceremonies at designated correctional facilities on holy days. After winning that case, the ACLU of Alabama represented some of the inmates again when the

State attempted to transfer them to a correctional facility in LouisIana that does not allow such religious ceremonies.[10]

Frequently, Southern states present the argument against sweat lodge ceremonies that sweat lodge ceremonies (Lakota, inipi) have not been a Southern Native tradition. This contradicts the well documented ancient practice of Southern tribes using sweat houses (Cherokee, â'si), which has extended deep into Mesoamerica (Nahuatl, temazcalli), and the growing contemporary practice of inipi ceremonies in the Southeast and beyond. The benefit of sweat lodge ceremonies is well-recognized. For example, a study of Aboriginal spiritual practices in CanadIans prisons, based on hundreds of interviews, including interviews with Elders, has documented the positive, life-changing impact of spiritual practices for Indigenous inmates, including sweat lodge ceremonies.[11]

Collectively, Native peoples also carry the burden of what is today identified as historical trauma. According to Lakota scholar Maria Yellow Horse Braveheart, "historical trauma is cumulative emotional and psychological wounding over the lifespan and across generations, emanating from massive group trauma. Native Americans have, for over 500 years, endured physical, emotional, social, and spiritual genocide from European and American colonialist policy. Contemporary Native American life has adapted, such that many are healthy and economically self-sufficient. Yet a significant proportion of Native people are not faring as well."[12] Historical trauma, which may often be an unrecognized cause of chronic stress, is seen as a major contributor to high suicide rates among young people, diabetes, heart disease, low birth weight, and other chronic diseases. Traditionally, post-traumatic stress disorder (PTSD) has been diagnosed and treated through ceremony. Navajo (Diné) name this disorder nayee (monster).[13] Nayee reaches into the institution of the United States legal system and incarceration practices as American Indian families negotiate caring for an imprisoned relative or as Native children attempt to make sense of the absence of a father, mother, or other close family members serving time. As many of the authors remember their childhood, parents are described as absent, chronically ill, abused by a spouse or intimate partner, or extremely stressed trying to provide food and shelter for their children. It is sometimes parents under duress who introduce their children to drugs, smoking and alcohol.

The United States has the highest documented imprisonment rate in the world. The majority of prisoners are between twenty and forty years of age, urban, and socioeconomically disadvantaged. According to the 2010 statistics of the US Bureau of Justice (BJS), state and federal authorities oversaw a prison population of over a million and a half men and women, or approximately one in two hundred US citizens, with an imprisonment rate of 497 inmates per 100,000.[14] In the same year, non-citizen inmates comprised 95,977 men and women in state facilities. The vast majority of inmates are serving time in state correctional institutions (1,395,356), and men constitute the largest imprisoned gender group (1,492,330). How does this high imprisonment rate relate to American Indian communities?

According to a 1997 study published by the BJS,

- At least seventy percent of the violent victimization experienced by American Indians is committed by persons not of the same race.
- American Indians experience per capita rates of violence of more than twice those of the U.S. resident population. Young people are especially vulnerable, with one in four men or women between eighteen and twenty-four years of age experiencing a violent crime.

- On a per capita basis, American Indians had a rate of prison incarceration about thirty-eight percent higher than the national rate.[15]

For the year 2008, the US Census Bureau reported that 1.01% of the population identified as American Indian or Alaska Native, 0.18% Native HawaiIan or Pacific Islander American, and 1.69% Multiracial American. The US prison population, however, was comprised of 6.06% American Indian, Alaska Native, Native HawaiIan, AsIan/Pacific Islander American, and Multiracial American inmates. In 2010, close to 80,000 American Indian and Alaska Natives were under correctional control nationwide, with the majority (two thirds) on probation or parole. A small percentage (a little over 2,000 inmates) was held in custody in BIA operated prison facilities on tribal land. Further impacting current penal issues are cultural differences and a complicated system of jurisdiction due to the separate spheres of state, federal, and tribal governmental authority in the prosecution of crimes, as well as the unreliability of crime statistics. It is estimated that at least half of crimes in American Indian communities go unreported. Among federally recognized tribes, tribal jurisdiction is limited, and efforts to bring back culturally based systems of correction, restorative justice, culturally based support for those who experienced crimes, Native ministry, and legislation encounter a great number of challenges.[16]

Given the high rate of incarceration, accurate knowledge about the families and communities affected by incarceration is essential yet difficult to find. As important as they are, prison statistics cover only part of the story, and tell us little about culture, religion, and the distinct legal situation of First Nations prisoners, their families, and their tribal nations. Such invisibility begins with government categories of racial identification. Although census forms identify American Indian, Alaska Native, Native HawaiIan and Pacific Islander background, other government statistical data may only distinguish between large groupings (white, black, Hispanic) that render Indigeneity under-documented and even invisible for both US citizen and non-citizen inmates. Indigenous peoples thus may be counted as generically "non-white" or not counted at all. It is also assumed that the three major groupings are "racially pure". However, not only are many American Indian and Alaska Native men and women part of a multi-ethnic family tree in red-black, red-yellow, and red-white, and with roots in Native HawaiIan and Pacific Islander cultures, but increasingly, "Hispanic" men and women reject the label as inaccurate and reclaim or proclaim their Indigenous identities as, for example, Taíno, Mixteka, Triqui, Azteka, or Mexikah.[17] As the essays in this collection demonstrate, in contrast to the divisions imposed by statistical data collection, life in First Peoples' communities in the South and beyond is clearly and strongly known as Indian, and fellow inmates administratively identified as "Hispanic" may be welcomed in the prayer circle as Indigenous brothers and sisters. However, Native identity takes on a different meaning behind bars than on the outside as the authors describe in their essays and poetry.

In areas where US census data identifies American Indian and Alaska Native communities specifically, the uniqueness of Indigenous social, cultural, and economic life becomes more tangible to non-Native audiences. Two historical forces have contributed to such uniqueness: one, the spiritual, cultural, and social strength of Native nations to remain true to themselves, and secondly, the five hundred year old Euro-American determination to occupy and have title to Indian lands.[18] For example, despite historical US government efforts to destroy Native languages, close to thirty percent of Native households have been able to hold on to speaking Native languages at home. Tribal efforts to strengthen and expand Indigenous language use are increasing daily. Even where English predominates, Indigenous languages have persisted to be spoken and remembered through the distinct words, phrases, and grammar used by the community.

Despite historical pressures to adapt to the nuclear family model typical of Euro-American culture, Indigenous households tend to be extended family networks rather than married-couple only households. Women often continue to hold informal and formal positions of leadership in the community as was the rule among many tribes before Euro-American systems spread sexism and patriarchal dominance.[19]

In the economic sector, First Nations men and women, despite an overall lower presence in the US labor force, have an above national average presence in farming, fishing, forestry, construction, extraction, and maintenance, the service sector, and production, transportation, and material moving professions.[20] Management, professional, and related work and sales and office jobs make up close to fifty percent of the overall work force. Although some tribes have made impressive economic and educational progress, Indigenous peoples' poverty rates overall are still disturbingly high and well below that of other groups. This fact is even more troubling when compared to pre-contact tribal well-being.[21] Running Water, one of the Brothers of the Buffalo, expressed his view on the current economic hardships as follows.

> First and foremost, the economy is not working. Too many political parties are only out for themselves, their own families, and money. Small businesses, retirement money, resources, human rights, and community development are all for sale. The US government is selling the American economy to other global economies for their mistakes. Families who have worked for so many years have nothing to show for it due to the fact that those who run the government take the workers' money to the rich. They leave families who live pay check to pay check with nothing. Even those in retirement have to go back to work due to the fact that the money in their retirement

> fund is gone.
>
> We as a people need to come together and have a government that gives to the American people, and not takes away from them. Stop selling American jobs to other global governments, put education first, uphold human rights, and make better decisions when spending money. This is a great country, but the decisions the government makes are unorganized, and hurt those who make this country grow. The people need to have a voice when it comes to selling jobs that keep America growing. The government needs to uphold the heritage that hard work pays off. It needs to have a better foreign policy when it comes to other global governments. I truly believe that if this government does not put education, hard work, and the people of this country first, then America will no longer be the land of the free.

As is true elsewhere, poverty allows a violence driven shadow economy to flourish that lacks sanction by laws and Indigenous justice traditions, even though it might be legal or at least quietly tolerated in US higher income domains (e.g., money laundering, trade in weapons and recreational addictive substances, prostitution). The human cost of legally unprotected economic shadow systems generated by poverty is unacceptable.

As noted above, American Indians suffer higher rates of exposure to violent crimes than any other ethnic group, and Native women, especially in urban areas, are experiencing intergenerational trauma of all forms of sexual abuse, including sexual trafficking. In the words of one American Indian female inmate, "We're all on the same path when we come to prison, on the road to self-destruction...The person we punish the most, hurt the most, when we come to prison is ourselves. The only common denominator I can break it down to is the pain. Most of it, I think, comes from abuse. I do believe, in my case, that abuse had something to do with my incarceration."[22] Spirituality, cultural expressions, and

Native pride offer potent protection against the physiological and emotional effects of historical trauma, and provide stamina on the road back to full self-determination. This book has been written in the spirit of Indian self-determination and communal healing, and testifies to the resilience of American Indian spiritual traditions beyond prison walls. Through poetry, the visual arts, and autobiography, it encourages others to rethink stereotypes and to imagine new ways of culturally based justice.

WHAT IF

Little Bull

What If I wasn't me?
What If I was someone else?
What if I did care about how someone felt?
What if I would have looked at life in a different view?
What if I would've stayed in school?
Do you think I would still have a chance
With that girl from the pool,
Who said she only like school boys and good dudes?
What if she would've just gotten to know the real me?
And found out that I'm not the bad guy that, that
People make me out to be.
What if these things really happened?
I guess if it would've,
Then "what if" wouldn't be the question.
What if I never came to prison at all?
What if I didn't, and
I never would've noticed my flaws.
What if it wasn't true that
Sometimes bad things happen for good reasons?
What if someone said that to you,
Would you believe it?

Now what if you were me and not someone else?
What if you was emotionally scarred, and
Didn't care who someone felt?
What if you saw life through my eyes, and
Not someone else?
Do you think you could've or would've made it
If you were me?
What if you had to quit school,
Just to help Grandma make ends meet?
What if you were twelve when you fell victim to the streets?

What If you were only five when both your Mom's and Pop's left?
Damn! Let me take a deep breath.
What if your dream of having a whole family was like a gun?
Wouldn't it be nice to conceal one?
What if you called the people you grew up with your family,
Because you never knew what it was like to have a real one?
What if my life wasn't hard?
What it if was easy?
What if I told you, "I've never had a problem in my whole life,"
Would you believe me?
"What if" is a question that is real deep.
So before you start to judge,
Think "what if" I were you and "what if" you were me.

TWO CROW FEATHERS

THANK THE CREATOR FOR TODAY

Two Crow Feathers

Thank the Creator for today
This is the beginning of a new day.
I can waste it or use it for good,
What I do today is important because I am exchanging a day of my life for it.
When tomorrow comes this day will be gone
Forever leaving in its place something I traded for it.
I want it to be gain not loss,
Good not evil,
Success not failure
In order I shall not regret the price I paid for today.

I keep this poem written and taped on the wall in my cell. Every day I wake, I read it and I say a prayer for the man who lost his life for which I serve this life sentence. I thank the Creator for allowing me to wake and walk upon Mother Earth and enjoy all He has given me. But it is another day. I have to wait to see Ian and tell him I am sorry for taking part in his death. Every day I get to join in on the road to the celebration of life, I carry a sadness with me.

I grew up in a small town in North Texas. I am half Comanche and half White. I grew up in and around Christianity and Traditional Ways. My Granny used to have to drag me to a Christian church, but my heart was true to traditional ways. Growing up, it was not good to be an Indian. My Dad used to tell me, "Son, never let anyone know you are Indian if you want to get anywhere in life." The people I grew up knowing were hateful and that burned into my heart. I grew up in bars, so drinking at an early age was normal for me. My mother left my Dad around 1980. She moved to South Florida. She grew up knowing it did not matter Indian or White, everybody's got to work. So by age fourteen, she was waitressing tables in a café in the 60's. She married my Dad when she was sixteen years old. By age seventeen, she was squeezing me out. She had three of us kids, me and two girls. My Dad, he retired from the military and opened a boot and shoe repair and Western stores. He also had a mobile boot and shoe repair and Western ware.

We did a lot of traveling. There was also a lot of heavy drinking and fighting. By the time they separated, it was for the good. My mother moved to South Florida and soon had a nice home, started her own business. Larry, who became my step father, had just started his business when he and my mother met prior to her leaving my Dad. I was back and forth from Texas to Florida. I watched my Mom work two and three jobs to make things work. She had a lot of struggles. I have seen her work so hard that her fingers bled and lose finger nails, go to work at five o'clock in the morning and go from one job to the next, working till ten to eleven o'clock at night, six days a week, and never did I hear her complain.

I spent a lot of time in South Texas and across the Border. Mainly Laredo Texas, across the border is Nuevo Laredo. I had a lot of connections, but the Family that used to control that city and the drugs was my main supply for whatever we wanted. I've seen buildings with so much coke cocaine and marijuana you could get it for almost nothing. Guns were my main thing. We had moved a lot of guns. Us Indians were strapped for war. In the 1980's, I had dealings with a motor cycle club in Texas. There were places set up throughout South Texas I would go to and party and make deals.

I met a man who just got out of the military. He told me about an Army base in Missouri where I could get my hands on anything, and the city cops were just as crooked. That was in 1991. In 1992, I went to check out Missouri. I spent three years there and I made the right connections. I had dealings within the military getting everything from M.R.E.s to weapons. I had gotten in good with a couple of dirty city and county cops, several motor cycle gangs and militias.

That whole time of my life I'd go to reservations and throughout the country where other Indians were and had sweat lodge and pipe ceremonies and Pow wows. I used to think I could be spiritually right and fight and do dirty dealings. In May of 1997, I found myself right in the middle of a murder. My sister had an ex-husband and one day he got killed. And I carried the murder charge. I got life without parole.

When Ian died, not only did his mother and father suffer and mourn, but my family as well. My mother and step father loved and thought the world of Ian. His son and daughter are my niece and nephew. I put a man in a fifty-five gallon drum, cased him in concrete. Every day since, I think about what had happened. I lost a family member and friend. I could have stopped his death. He would be here today. But I didn't take someone seriously enough till it was too late. Thirteen years, June 4th, that's how long I've been locked up.

The first couple of years in prison, I had a hard time accepting non-Indians coming to the prayer circle. In fact, I hated it because most of them only came there to get beads and leather and a sense of protection. North Carolina was and is a strange place to me. But I realized one day that in order for my spirituality to grow, I could not worry myself over the small things. I had to concentrate on my own old self through spirituality. I had to serve an eviction notice to my old way of thinking. Sometimes my old way of thinking wants to move back in. I try not to be my old self and I work hard to maintain a peaceful balance within myself.

The "Red Road" as we have come to call it, and the sacred circle give me the balance and peace within. I spend a lot of time connecting myself with nature and the spirits to make myself a stronger and better person. I use this time in prison to do just that. A lot of people come to prison and not accomplish anything to better their selves. I've seen prison break a man down, mentally and physically. A person with a weak mind will not make it through prison. Many lose their minds, their will, and even their life. There is an old saying, "only the strong survive." That is very true.

Even though I lost my freedom and I am physically locked up in prison, I am free. In my mind, I have set myself free. Spiritually speaking, the chains that bind me physically are not long and strong enough to contain my mental and spiritual self. Being American Indian and a traditionalist walking this sacred road and circle is my life. I teach those who truly want to become better human beings a sacred and spiritual way of life. A lot of people think that only the prayer pipe is what makes a sacred ceremony. But there is a lot more to it, from the drum and songs, the smudging, the way we enter and pray, to the way we exit. Everything is done in a sacred way. Everything is done in a spiritual ceremony way.

Some people think that all they have to do is learn how to handle a pipe and they think they know everything. I can go to the zoo and get a pet monkey and teach him to handle a pipe, but does that monkey know the spiritual reason of the pipe? No! People are the same way. To understand the spirituality of things, the way we walk this sacred road, this Red Road, you have to make sacrifices. You have to erase all the things you think you know and start over. You have to serve an eviction notice on your old way of thinking. Walking this sacred road is an everyday way of life, not just from the time you wake up till you go to bed, but even when you sleep. There are the trickster spirits that come to you at night and slip into your dreams. So you got to be ready for them at all times. The spirit beings do not rest and that includes the one that resides within you.

Even though my spirituality is growing, I do not like to think of myself as getting old. But who does. I'm in my early forties and I don't think I've come close to reaching Elder Status or consider myself an Elder. Even though I teach others, I just pass on some wisdom and knowledge that was handed down to me.

Helping others helps me spiritually. The time of writing this is at the same time as the oil leak in the Gulf of Mexico. The Blunder of B.P., I call it. I see the images on TV of birds covered in oil so badly they can't even move and it breaks my heart, knowing that no one really cares. The news will use it to boost their ratings and politicians will use it against each other to gain a foot hold in Washington. The ones who suffer are the animals and the working people who provide not only food for their families, but for everyone else.

When I pray, I pray for the ones who suffer, the ones who are sick. I give thanks to the Creator for all He has given me. Even the hardships I have encountered, because if it wasn't for the hardships and pain, I would not understand the values of life.

Sometimes I wonder why I am still alive. When I was running around out on the streets, I put myself in dangerous situations on a daily basis. I've been in bar room brawls and to shoot outs. I've made friends and plenty of enemies. But for some reason, the Creator needed me to remain alive a lot longer than I thought I would.

Coming to prison: did it save my life or someone else's? I do not know, but what I do know is I don't think the Creator wants me to sit around and use this time to just entertain myself. I try to pay close attention to everything. The Creator guides my path and I do my best to be honest and helpful and to be there for anyone who needs me.

I also spend a lot of times alone, kind of in a meditation state. Trying to connect with the Spirits and the Creator. Watching, listening for wisdom, knowledge, guidance and a message, a vision. Every time, I gain a little of everything. You have to pay attention or it will pass you by. I love to drum or even to chant songs or to play a flute (Native American wood flutes). Those are other ways I use to pray and meditate. I am very thankful the Creator has given me the gift of musical talent.

I am also very thankful for my family and the friends who have stuck with me on this long hard journey. Real good friends like Charlie in England and Billy and Jan, who are like my own family to me. Charlie is a very good hearted person who cheers me up with his letters. He has sent me many pictures of castles and towns and ancient places in England. My Escarrio brother Billy and his wife Jan and daughter Mary, who write me letters. Good people. And my family, my mother and my father, all of them could have gone on with their lives and left me in the past as a distant memory. But they stood with me and their love and kindness helps my spirituality grow.

Some people go through life looking for earth-shaking, mountain-moving miracles only to grow old and empty, when all along it's in the small tiny forms that we pass by every day. If you stop to take notice, those small and tiny miracles will add up to be earth-shaking and mountain-moving miracles.

Three weeks ago, the Prison Chaplain informed me that my father had passed away. He had been ill for almost eleven months. He went in for surgery on his lower back and died. The doctors had to revive him. They said he was not going to live and put him in Hospice. But he held on. Then they put him in a nursing home. He just could not fully recover. I have sadness in my heart. I will miss him. He was an eighty nine years old retired military man. The military buried him with full honors. What saddens me is that I could not be there for him when he needed me or even go to the funeral, because I am in a North Carolina prison. But I honor him and say thank you. He is in the Spirit World now. The Spirit World is what gives us strength. I give honor to a man who loved to live life. Even in times of death and sadness, I use that knowledge to form my spirituality and spiritual growth. It's like connecting the dots.

If you take the star constellations map, lines draw out symbols. We really never pay them any mind. But if you stop, study and ponder on it, how did humankind knew thousands of years ago what to look for? What kind of technology unknown at the time did they possess? How did they know to connect the stars to make shapes and forms? It was not alien or secret advanced technology. The technology they had does supersede any technology of today and tomorrow. In fact, that piece of technology has been around since humankind first started: spiritual growth and the willingness to stop, study and ponder on it.

In today's world, there is too much distraction. The other day, a young man, twenty-three years old, just came to prison. We were watching Discovery. Apparently he had never seen the Discovery Channel, because he was simply amused to learn that bees make honey. His mind is only knowledgeable about what size of tire is on a car or what size of speaker or brand of stereo or who got the best rap album. But he knows nothing about life and doesn't really care to change. It is sad, because he is not the only one. There are many, many more just like him. They care nothing about life or spirituality, they care only about technology.

I give thanks to the Creator for giving me a good brain and the will to change my life to be a better person, to know when to stop, study and ponder on life. I knew this my whole life. But I let the distractions of technology interfere and I forgot to stop, study and ponder. Now I serve a life sentence.

I have met really good brothers of the same sacred path I walk and we have become Brothers of the Buffalo. We have bonded, we have sacrificed and shared each other's lives, wisdom, knowledge and love. We have helped each other's spiritual growth. And even though we go different ways on our paths throughout the prison system, we are always spiritually connected through the sacred circle, this sacred Red Road we walk.

This book project, *Brothers of the Buffalo Speak Up*, I am very proud and honored to be a part of it with Brothers I have known for many years. To me this is more than just a book, and it's not just about individuals. We are family and have shared our lives with each other and the world. Sharing my life story and spiritual ways I am honored to do.

The sacred pipe is my life. When I smoke my pipe with someone, I share my life with them. The sacred circle and the sacred pipe: it is more than just a spiritual belief. It is more than just a way of life: it is our past, our presence, our future, our blood. It is everything on this Mother Earth, everything in all of space, everything in the spirit world.

Today, I thank the Creator for allowing me to wake and walk upon Mother Earth another day. Chief Ten Bears of the Numunuu Comanche people once gave a speech. He spoke the words that are born in my heart:

> I was born upon the Prairie where the wind blew free and there was nothing to break the light of the sun. I was born where there were no enclosures and where everything drew a free breath. I want to die there and not within walls.
>
> Chief Ten Bears, Numunuu Comanche[23]

WHEN I DIE

Little Bull

When I die don't cry,
Celebrate.
For I get a new start.
I'm not gone forever,
It's just for now that we depart.
My blood will be gone,
My wind will be out,
But I will still be here.
Not in the physical sense,
But as a spirit, know that I will still be near.

STILL STANDING: "NOT THE SAME IN COLOR"

Jarrod
African Native American, One of the Buffalo Brothers

Here are five questions, some food for thought before you begin reading my life story.

Influence is Power

Can you change your view of me with a look at my hazel eyes?
Will you judge me or portray me as I am?
If you don't like or even understand what I represent, will you condemn your own faith by passing judgment on mine?
If my God isn't like your God, and I don't believe what you believe, will you discredit my spirituality, or worse, will you try to convince others to believe that I am a plague on mankind, with no goals or use?
Do I have to describe fear to prove that I am scared?

I know who I am. And I am who I am. We all have a life story to tell, and I got a right to tell mine. March the 5th 1978, Ms. Betty Jean R., the oldest daughter out of seven children of African American woman Christine R. and Native Haliwa-Saponi (American Indian) male Mr. Charlie L.R., gave birth to her fifth child, me, Jarrod, out of six children. What I'm about to say will make some white Americans and Native Americans unhappy, furious, mad and never will they acknowledge me, because racism still lives in all segments of American society today. More than likely, I will never be accepted or have a chance registering as an African-Native American because of racism. Still today, people look at me, and say "you don't look like an Indian." All in all, I say, you don't know me, my family, or my bloodline. A lack of cultural racial teaching keeps American people ignorant today. People think that American Indians are red or white or colored people, but I love to give these people notice that there are African-Native Americans in America today who walk the Medicine Wheel faithfully like me. Wow! And by the way, I used to get a lot of slaps on the face, because I would fall asleep in church. As one, Native people are good people! As one, African people are good people!

When I was young, the only thing I knew about Native American Indians was what I had seen on TV: "cowboys and Indians." You know, in Hollywood they give Native American people a bad image. That image says, Native American people are bad, savage people. White people are good people, and "blacks", African people, are not good, are worthless people. I am Native and African. I always knew I had Indian blood in me, because my mother and grandfather looked like the Indians on TV. At first, when I started walking the Medicine Wheel, a lot of people would say, "Hey – you don't look like no Indian – you look black as the bottom of my boot". Little did they know that I have Native blood in me. Yes, I'm brown or black as the bottom of a boot, but I am very proud to have this skin color, and I shine it up and wear this skin color "happily" every day. People have seen full blooded Indians. People have seen white mixed Indians. People really haven't seen an African-Native American. I'm here. This is me talking! I have read a lot of books and seen a lot of films on great Chiefs, but I have not seen one film or read one book on an African-Native American -- so do we not exist? Maybe one day, I will read a book or see a film on an African-Native person or maybe that day will never come. Honestly, I haven't seen a picture of an African-Native American, but I do see one every time I look in the mirror. All Native American Indians are not the same in color of race as you have seen on TV or read in books. A lot of people will not admit it, but you have many African-Native Americans like myself. I walk the Medicine Wheel like a red or white man. Food for thought. This African Native American Buffalo is still standing for life.

For Christine R. aka Grandma (1934 -2004): A Poem

We Know You are Free

Grandma, we know your body and spirit are free
You don't have to be frail anymore.
We know you are free.
You don't have to agonize about us anymore,
You don't have to urgently petition no more.
We know you are free, no more adultery, and hospitals.
We know your body and spirit are free.
I will never ignore your spirit or forget your love,
and all the things that you have done for me.
Your family will never stop loving you.
We will always need you by our side, but Grandma,
the Great Spirit saw fit for you to give up your fight.
So He came,
and carried His special angel home.
So now we know you are free!!!

Most times, my Grandma and I didn't see eye to eye, and that's all I'll say, but her first daughter Betty Jean gave one hundred percent and more in raising me, my non-communication sister and my two late brothers. So I guess you can say, I want to thank my grandmother for giving me my mother. At the end of the day, thank you, Christine R.

As for growing up, I don't remember much as a child, because there was not much to remember. My household in childhood was poor. At the end of the month, some nights I went to bed hungry because there was no food. At the beginning of the month, I was so happy and full-bellied because that's when the American government hands out food stamps. We lived in government housing, "the projects." I do remember a time when I was living in the Rocky Mount, Nash County of N.C., projects.

My other two brothers and I only had four pairs of pants between us. That was when my life was really hard for me and my family. My mother raised six children by herself. She was the mother, the father, the Tooth Fairy, the Easter Bunny, and Santa Claus all in one. My mother Betty used to ask me, did I smoke cigarettes. I was twenty years old before I admitted that I smoked cigarettes. The story of my first cigarette: I was with my brother-in-law and his cousin. My brother-in-law's cousin got a new car and we were riding and drinking beer. Yes, I was tipsy as could be, but I wasn't drunk. My brother-in-law was in the passenger seat. His cousin was driving and I was in the back seat, tipsy. My brother-in-law's cousin was smoking a cigarette. I saw the red cherry of the cigarette and I took the cigarette out of my brother-in-law's mouth and I started smoking it and I got really high. So after that day, every time I drank beer, I smoked cigarettes. Then I got to the point where I didn't drink beer, but I still smoked cigarettes. I make a long story short. I started smoking cigarettes a long time ago, but as of seven months ago from today, I don't smoke cigarettes anymore. I quit smoking forcefully, because N.C. D.O.C. doesn't allow tobacco products on state property anymore, and by me being in prison, tobacco products are illegal.

I haven't seen my mother or anyone in my family since the year 2005, but I still feel my mother's love. Yes, there were times when Christmas came, but Santa Claus didn't come to our apartment; my birthday was just another day, but in a lot of ways, my mother made up for it. She's a reason why I'm still standing.

My mother is very, very sick, and she is all I got. I'll understand that when the Great Spirit comes and gets her spirit, her spirit will always be with me and in me. My mother doesn't want me to know she's sick, but I know.

Mother and I know where the Brothers of the Buffalo and I stand. We stand as one for one another, with love and respect. When I sent my mother a photo of me and my Brothers of the Buffalo, she wrote me back saying "you and your family look good and strong in there." I was so happy when I read that in one of the last letters my mother wrote to me.

In Loving Memory of Mr. Charlie Lee R. (1930-2004):
A Poem

It's Hard Letting Go

Letting go is one of the hardest things to do.
In life comes a time when you have to let all your feelings and spirit show.
My Grandfather "Big Charlie" is the man.
I love him and he truly loves me, that's why I'm still so sad.
He has endured a lot of pain.
He has fought battles and he has won.
He's peacefully now with the Great Spirit.
I will always and forever miss him.
I'll never stop thinking of him.
The thought of knowing that he will be in this wonderful and gracious place is the only reason I am letting go.
Love always,
Preacher and the Grandchildren

My grandfather was a wonderful Native man and a hell of a poker player. If I was asked about his card playing ability or luck, and his love for me, I would say,

"Can't nobody beat that big Haliwa-Saponi Indian in a card game." The love that he and my step grandmother Dorothea R. showed and gave me was unconditional. This is the other reason why I'm still standing. I don't know who gave me the nickname "Boggie", but Charlie and Dorothea wore it out. I want to thank Charlie Lee R. for having given me my mother.

I don't talk about my father because I really don't know him. He was never there for me, but even though I'm in prison, I am still standing. His name is James. I want to give acknowledgement to some of the names of my family lineage, the Richardson, Allen, Taylor, Mill, Joyner, Gupton, Vick, Lee, Lucas, and for my little baby sister's family, the Morris lineage.

About my brothers Eric and Derrick. One day, my brother Eric and I went to this church healing service thing at the armory in Spring Hope NC right across the street where we used to live in a big white house with government assistance. The white house used to be where the Spring Hope, NC Fire Department sits now. At this church healing service, I remember the preacher hollering. The collection plate kept coming around and I was like, "I'm not going to keep giving up my candy money." My brother Eric elbowed me in the side, and said, "The money will help people, so give it up." So I put all my little money in the collection plate. Now I'm sitting there all crazy looking as a child, thinking, "What I'm going to do about my candy money?" The collection plate came around again, and I guess my brother had seen the look on my face, because he looked me dead in my face and my eyes and told me I better not start acting up in here, and he pulled out a dollar and asked a blind man that sat beside us, did he have change for a dollar. The blind man reached in his pants pocket and pulled out a handful of change, and I jumped up and yelled out, "Hallelujah, we're rich." My brother Eric gave me a look that said, "I'm going to beat your butt". When we got home, I sat my butt down, and kept my mouth shut. The blind man moved his hand full of change toward Eric and Eric got four quarters, and he gave the blind man the dollar. Eric gave me two of the four quarters. The collection plate was passed down and Eric put his two quarters in the collection plate and he was trying to pass the collection plate to me. I turned my head, and started looking at the ceiling holding on to them two quarters for dear life – but something told me to look down the row. There is Grandma Christine sitting, looking down the row straight at me. I didn't even remember putting the two quarters in the collection plate, and passing it, but I do remember acting like I was paying attention for the rest of the night. The preacher started calling people up front for healing and I remembered the same blind man was sitting beside us, who gave us the change for a dollar, went up to the preacher. The preacher asked the blind man what was wrong. The blind man said he was blind. The preacher put his hand over the blind man's eyes and started shaking, saying words that I didn't understand. Then the blind man fell to the ground and I'm like, "What the heck." The blind man got up and said that he could see the light and I'm thinking, "Wow."

Then the preacher pointed at my Grandma and my Grandma pointed at my brother Eric. Eric got up from his chair and walked up to the preacher. The preacher asked Eric what is wrong. Eric said, "I have asthma". The preacher put his hand on Eric's chest and did his hollering in more words I did not understand, and stopped, and told my brother he was healed by God and told Eric to run up and down the alley. That time, Eric ran, no problem. But before I was in my teens, Eric aka Pookie passed away, right in front of me and my mother. I will never forget that night. Eric was always sick. He had a chronic disease, asthma. As I speak in writing right now, I'm crying, because it still hurts inside. As if it were yesterday, I still see my brother Eric laying on the ground dead and my mother laying on the porch crying and me standing there crying, saying, "The preacher said God healed him. The preacher said God healed Eric". I will take that night with me to my grave.

My brother Derrick aka Weasel died before I got out of the ninth grade. It hurts in places inside of me that

I didn't know that feelings could hurt in. My brother Derrick's passing still hurts today. Derrick and I were hanging out for the weekend. You see, Derrick had a hearing problem. He went and graduated from the N.C. School of the Deaf in Wilson, NC. In my ninth grade year, Derrick and I were hanging out. Yes, we were drinking and smoking weed. Sunday came and Derrick brought me back home where my mother and baby sister stayed in Franklinton, NC, in an apartment on 207 Hawkins St. Before Derrick left, he told me that he had to do something, and by the time I would get out of school Monday, he would take me to go get some shoes. Yes, shoes and music was my and Derrick's thing that we liked together.

Monday, I was in school, and my school principal got me and my sister out of class and told us, "Your mother will come and pick you up." I knew something was wrong because of the look on the principal's face. My mother picked us up, and we went to the store where she worked part time called "Snack Shack". When she got out of the car, the police told my mother she needs to go to Fayetteville, because my brother Derrick was in a car wreck. My mother asked the police was he okay and the police didn't answer (please excuse my hand writing but I'm crying). After the police didn't answer, my mother understood and the look and the worry she had on her face...I couldn't look at my mother's face, because of the hurt that she had on her face. My mother didn't cry right in front of me and my sister because she was being strong for us. Till this day, I still see the hurt in my mother's eyes losing her two sons. We all know the saying, a mother knows when something's wrong with her child, but a child knows when something's wrong with his or her mother, too.

Jarrod, me, the only son my mother has left, on drugs – nobody tried to help me get off drugs. I don't know how I got hooked on beer, drugs, and stealing. I was in and out of prison. As far as stealing is concerned, it was a disease, a rush I had to have. Beer, stealing, and drugs in my body system – there was no high like it. Nothing in this little story is about me, just about my wrongdoings. The life of being forlorn by choice, drugs by choice, and crime by choice will lead to two places: prison or death. *Non compos mentis*, it could lead to both: "died in prison." If you want to know more about me or my way of life, write and just ask me. I'm in a NC prison. I have done a lot of wrong things in my past, but I never stole anything from anyone in my family. I stole from someone else's family, and that was even worse. Today I am serving fifteen to eighteen years in NC prisons, not for the second degree murder charge listed on the computer, but for all the things that I have done wrong in my past. I know for a fact that I could have beaten the murder charge that was on me. If anyone will look it up, you will find no evidence against me. I pleaded guilty to the plea, not the murder charge.

When I put myself in prison, I was tired of my life and the only good thing that could come out of my life at that time was death. I hate to say it, but I'm one of these people – prison saved my life. Out of all these years, I can finally look in the mirror and say, I forgive you, Jarrod. Put all the B.S. aside. A person has to forgive him or herself first, and really mean it before that person can ask for forgiveness from all the people he or she has done wrong.

The Native way of spiritual living is not a religion. It is a way of life. That means that I endure, that I love and respect life. The men I walk the Medicine Wheel with are the only family I have. I guess that saying "out of sight, out of mind" is true, because my household family is either too busy to take at least five minutes to write me back, or my household family has forgotten about me, or my household family has written me off because I'm in prison. I don't know what the deal is between my household family and me. I don't know where we stand. I try and I do write them. My sisters don't write me back. Aunts, uncles and cousins: I don't know any of their addresses, but more than likely, they wouldn't write me back either. Don't get me wrong: I have tried the pen-pal thing, but when a pen-pal finds out by me telling her that I get out of prison in 2019, they stop writing.

When I first came to prison, my life had no meaning. I was always depressed and mad at the world because of no reason. I have broken laws and it's my fault. I put myself in prison, no one else did. Even though I'm a lonely man, I'm at peace with myself now for the first time in my life. I haven't seen anyone in my household family since I came to prison. Yes, I haven't had a visitor yet. Yes, I do get sad and my feelings are hurt, but I have to keep moving on with my life. Just like the Medicine Wheel. I have to keep moving forward.

I have read the Bible, I have read the Qur'an. Please do not misunderstand me. I respect all religions and ways of life, but I got nothing out of it. I will never put down a person's way of life, but when the Great Spirit calls on me to walk the Wheel, it's like telling my heart just to be truth, sacred spiritual love, happiness, beatitude. It's the best thing that has happened in my life. For the first time in my life, as I can remember, I feel alive.

A person here has to have some type of spiritual uplift to stay alive. I am not a perfect man, and I'll be the first to tell you that, but I am a better man than I was five years ago. I am a better man than I was one year ago. I am a better man than I was one day ago. Why? Because I want to be a better person, a good person to and for the people I come in contact with. How? I tell you. The Great Spirit. As I get older, spiritually I look at life differently and I cannot believe the things I have done in the past. When I look back on my life, I ask myself "boy, what in the world were you thinking?" and I can never answer it. Now, I do not lie or sell anyone dreams, because I don't buy any.

I have played every game of life there is to be played. With me, the playing of games is over. I do not play games with people anymore, because I don't want anyone playing games with me. People say that the truth hurts. Well, I say, let it hurt and tell the truth. I speak with my own voice. I have nothing to hide. I journeyed to some evil places. Life is the journey I'm on now.
The "Red Road" is for life. It isn't easy for someone to find their own way of life spiritually. Be true with yourself and others. It is what it is, but life can and will get better.

As far as for my own future, the only thing I can promise is that I will still be walking the Great Medicine Wheel, making myself a better person one day at a time. As far as for my household family and me, I don't know. It's up in the air, but I'm open minded and understanding.

Jarrod Christopher L. is a Brother of the Buffalo, African-Native American in heart, mind, spirit, and blood. Some people don't believe it, but destiny rules us all. It's what you want to do with the hand you were dealt. Good or bad, but, people, don't fold. Thrive to be better persons mentally, spiritually, and physically.
Lead by example, guaranteeing the survival of all.
Influence is power, so what we do in life and what we say matters.
Remember, in the end, we cannot fool ourselves.
Be true to yourself and others, and let's live together.

Still standing, not the same in color.

TODAY

Red Horse

Today is a new day.
Yesterday is gone.
We must allow hurt and pain to move on.
We must smile, for today is a new day.
Go outside, feel the sun, and smell the earth.
Allow the wind to blow through your soul as you let the tears flow.

Snow Hawk

MORE THAN ONE WAY OF SEEING

Snow Hawk

Greetings, my brothers, sisters, uncles, nephews, grandmothers, grandfathers, and all my relations! I hope these words travel many winds and stir your spirit. I wish that I could leave just something small from Grandfather that would help someone on this earthly walk.

I was born in 1972 on Seymour Johnson Air Force Base in Goldsboro, NC. My parents moved to an Air Force base in Michigan where I spent the first six years of my life. Even though I was very young, I remember the huge snows and the big grasshoppers while picking fresh blueberries in the summer. At around six years old, we moved back to North Carolina to be close to family. We never had much, but Mom and Dad always made sure we made it with what we needed. Most of the time they were struggling to find work, which was not easy to find in the mid-70s. When possible, often two jobs were worked. I learned at a young age how to work in the garden and pull my weight around the house, but I wasn't alone, my little sister was right there with me. Of course I was mean as a snake and picked on her all the time, but I was also very protective of her. Being a young stubborn boy and her brother gave me special picking privileges that no one else was allowed to partake in. But my sister and I are pretty close.

Sometime in the 80's our parents divorced. My sister went with my Mom and I stayed with my Father. Times got a little harder, but we stuck together and got by. I always spent a lot of time with my grandparents on both sides of the family, who were showing me nothing but love and teaching me many things about life, respect, and doing right. They instilled in me ethics and morals such as working hard and caring for family, and being the best at everything that you do. My Papaw's (Grandfather's) motto was "do it right or don't do it all"! I learned a great deal from this good man I call Papaw, a man extremely loyal to family, with rich family values. He is a fiddle player, raised in the country, and living on a farm. And he continues to live this lifestyle to this day. He taught me all about working. From digging ditches to mowing grass, working on fences, building retainer walls, a little roofing, carpentry of all kinds, chopping wood, mixing concrete, running wire, painting, caulking the whole cabin, using the tractor, planting, weeding, and harvesting. He always finds something that needs to be done without much thought.

In our spare time, we would enjoy learning about wildlife, and how to track, read signs and hunt. But we never hunted anything around the house, so the wildlife continued to come around. We would see deer every day, an occasional bear, and fox. We had several dens of foxes over the years. I really enjoyed and continue to enjoy nature and wildlife probably more than anything. As I got a little older, I spent almost all of my free time fishing, hiking, camping and hunting. Nothing compares to the beauty of the mountains and a wild trout stream, or a beautiful lake. One of my uncles who recently crossed over had a houseboat on Fontana Lake near the Cherokee Reservation in North Carolina. I spent many a great summer as a young kid with my cousin on that lake. I miss my uncle and our fish fry's, those were good times!

When I was growing up, my Great Grandmother on my Dad's side told me that we had Cherokee in our family lineage, and I have always had some kind of inclination and wondering about the Indian way of life. It took years before I started really getting involved in and learning the truth about these ways, which we will cover shortly. Unfortunately, during my teens, I spent time running the roads doing drugs, drinking like a fish, and getting into a lot of trouble.

Eventually, I started selling drugs, enjoying the

money being made, and the exciting fast life that came along with it. Lots of money, lots of women, lots of drugs, lots of so-called friends, and lots of stupid decisions that I am paying for today. My life was a mess as I found myself always fighting, receiving several assault charges, some minor drug offenses, plus a few larceny charges.

Every time I went to Court, I would plead to a lesser charge or plead guilty so I could get out quick and get back to the party. This went on for years. I was lucky to never get caught with a large amount of drugs. Life was good, or so I thought at the time. What I did not realize is that all these guilty pleas that I accepted kept raising my prior record level points. This increased my prison sentence due to the structured sentencing laws of North Carolina. I've already been to prison three times, and I'm doing now a thirty-six-year sentence, wondering what happened.

Because of the life and the path that I have chosen, I am now thirty-eight years of age and I have thirty-two years of incarceration to go. One day, I was talking to a White Mountain Apache. I told him of my Cherokee lineage. He was a really good guy, and carried himself really well. Come to find out he was the pipe keeper and prayer leader of the Native American circle at Alexander Prison in 2006. He kept urging me that if I was interested to come and talk to the guys and check it out sometime.

So one day I decided to see what it was like, even though you would hear negative comments in the yard. Others were laughing about smoking the pipe and drum playing. All they saw was people playing Indian like on TV. I went out anyway and one of the Brothers sat outside the ceremony circle with me and explained the significance of the pipe and ceremony. I remember smelling the sacred herbs (smudge) for the first time. It immediately awakened something within me that seemed real and familiar. I was surrounded by peace. For the first time in years, my mind left the prison, went outside the walls. It was almost unexplainable, but I will never forget it. It started pulling me toward that way of life (the Red Road) and is still pulling me as I write these words. I was still getting write-ups and was full of anger at the hand life had dealt me, but I switched my religion to Native American in 2007 and started really learning about this way of life, also about the ceremonies, the beliefs.

I started digging deep into history. The more I dug, the more I found out that just about everything that I was taught in school about Indians and our history was a lie, and the more it troubled me about the fate of my people. The genocide, hate, greed, murdering of innocent elders, women, and children, the decimation of the Buffalo, one of the final plots to destroy the main food supply in order to drive the Red Man out of his natural state of livelihood, and to be destroyed once and for all, only because of the greed for land and natural resources.

The Indians and the land, the trees, the plants, the four legged, the two legged, the winged, the creepy crawlers, the sky, Mother Earth, air, water, fire, are all related. They are one and part of each other. One cannot exist without the other. Take one away and the rest will die. We need each other to survive.

The white man never understood the Indian people and their ways. They still don't, but they are learning. Still, there are great waters to be crossed, along with trust to be earned. The indigenous peoples of this continent (Turtle Island) were considered devil worshipers, heathens, and savages who could not be tamed and had to bow to the will and the ways of the white man's religions or be destroyed, enslaved, and formed into the image of the Europeans at all cost. All that the whites saw were untapped resources and opportunity for the taking.

The Indian was willing to share the land with the whites. The Indian way of thinking was that no man could sell or own what belonged to the Great Spirit. But the white man's greed was too great to live harmoniously with others and respect their ways and beliefs.

The Indians had no word for religion. They had a close relationship with all of creation, working in harmony and in balance with nature, the elements, and Grandfather, the Great Spirit. All things that the Creator's hand is seen in are sacred. Every step, every breath, every day. It is a way of life referred to as Walking the Good Red Road (or the Medicine Path). It is a simple way of life which makes complete sense.

Today, we have Brothers from all four directions, different tribes from all over the United States, Canada, and Mexico. Just to name a few: Cherokee, Lumbee, Lakota, Taíno, Mayan, Wampanoag, Comanche, and Apache. Whether Red, Yellow, Black, or White, we all come together as equals on common ground to send a voice as one to that which is Great and Mysterious. As a traditional practice, some tribes use the Sacred Pipe. The bowl is the Earth, the stem is everything that grows on the Earth, the grains of tobacco represent all the Powers and all that there is in the Universe.

So the Pipe is the universe. Each grain of tobacco is part of our relations and they sacrifice their self to the fire for the Creator. The Pipe is also man and his own center as well. So we become as one with the six directions and with that which is holy. The bowl also represents the heart of man. The smoke represents the invisible breath. The bowl is usually made out of catlinite pipestone (or bloodstone) and is only found at the pipestone quarries in Pipestone, Minnesota. The smoke carries our prayers with the help of the spirit of Hawk and Eagle to the Great Spirit in the Sky Vault (the Creator). These things are very sacred. Many herbs have been used for thousands of years for healing, purifications, medicines, paints, and many other uses that we give thanks for.

To name a few of the most common: Sage, Cedar, Sweet Grass, Tobacco, Juniper, Copal, and even Lavender. The pipe is not only an extension of the body, but also an extension of the spirit as well, in direct line and contact with the Great Spirit. This is a deeply spiritual belief that we share. One cannot see it from the outside looking in or fully understand it without the experience itself. Through much prayer, meditation, and working in the four directions we try to achieve balance in the mental, spiritual, emotional, and physical states of mind, body, and consciousness.

I have managed to turn my life around through this belief and way of life. I am now off all the mental health medications I have been on for the last eighteen years for bipolar, depression, anxiety, and panic attacks. The more I started feeling sluggish, the more I tried to achieve balance and the less meds I took. Eventually, I came all the way off. I knew that to achieve the things I wanted, I needed my mind in its entirety. Through prayer and volition, I slowly came off the medications. Never losing a night's sleep and needing them again. The change has been unbelievable. Also, I have let go of all of that anger and hatred. I've learned forgiveness, acceptance, love, the importance of family, and other things that I have taken for granted all these years. I've learned to achieve my goals: more than one way of seeing things, understanding how my actions and words might affect others before I even do them.

Don't get me wrong. I am far from perfect and I still make bad decisions sometimes and mistakes also, but I try to learn from them and move on. We are all going to make mistakes. We are not perfect. We are human. I've obtained a greater respect for my life and all living things. I give thanks for the lessons I have learned today and dedicate a portion of my efforts to the benefit of all.

I try to learn patience, humility, kindness, and to keep an open mind. It is hard, but these are all keys to a better way of life and of peace within. I have learned a very small portion of this knowledge and way of life, but the impact of it has changed my life and my thoughts astronomically. I will carry this way of life with me always.

When you pick up the pipe, it is for life! The love and respect I have been gifted with from some of my

Brothers is indescribable and different from anything I have ever known. We are family and kindred spirits. The Brothers will always have a place very close to my heart. I give thanks to Grandfather (Creator) for my relations and this way of life. I have learned to go within myself and learn who I really am.

Pure spirit of love and light: this is our connection and path to all that was, all that is, and all that ever will be. It has no beginning and no end, it just simply is. Not unlike the Great Spirit himself. When I hold my sacred feather, I am reminded of the power of prayer and the power of nature and I give thanks.

So it is good. I like when Vine Deloria Jr. states in his book *God is Red*, "Tos-Ga-oo-wee-aych-ton is an ancient word meaning 'to make it right.' You must always seek to restore things to balance as you leave. There is no sin or guilt on the medicine path, but we must repay all debts, resolve all misunderstandings, and fix what is broken before we move on. That is why there are no 'Native American Express Cards'." Whenever something is taken, you always give something back.

Lakota Pipe Song

by Henry Crow Dog[24]

Friend of the Eagle, to you I pass the pipe first
Around the circle I pass it to you
Around the circle to begin the day
Around the circle I complete the four directions
I pass the pipe to the Grandfather above
I smoke with the Great Mystery
So begins a good day.

Here is a re-telling of a Cherokee traditional story.[25]

Story of the First Fire

In the beginning there was no fire. The world was very cold. One day, a long time ago, the Thunders who lived in the sky sent their lightning and put fire into the bottom of a hollow sycamore tree that grew on the island. The animals knew the fire was there, because they could see the smoke coming out at the top of the tree, and they wanted to warm themselves. But they could not get to it because of the water. So they held a council to decide what to do. Every animal that could fly or swim was eager to get the fire. Vulture or "Suli" in Cherokee, was the largest of the birds and was greatly admired for his wonderful plume he had on his head.
When the moment arrived, everyone turned to him with expectant faces. He flew up to the tree and captured one ember of the flame. With nowhere else to put it, he placed it on his head and wrapped it in his beautiful plumage. On the way back, he smelled something burning. The smell got stronger and stronger. Suddenly he felt a burning sensation on his head, and he screamed out, "Ahhhgh! I've been burned." He shook his head and the ember fell into the water and turned to smoke with a great fizzling sound. When he arrived back on dry land, everyone was staring at him with shock. He felt the top of his head. His beautiful plumage, the pride of his clan, was gone. He was bald! Raven offered to go because he was so large and strong and smart, all the others thought he should go next. They all admired him for his beautiful feathers of many colors.

He flew high and far across the water and, alighting on the sycamore tree, gazed at the flame, wondering what to do. While he was thinking and thinking, the heat scorched all his feathers black, and he became frightened and flew away. He arrived back at the gathering of disappointed animals empty handed, without any fire. They were shocked to see his beautiful feathers turned black. Sharp eyed little Screech Owl volunteered to go. He reached the island safely, but while he was looking down into the hollow tree, a blast of hot air came up and nearly burned out his eyes. He flew home as fast as he could, but it was a long time before he could see well. The eyes of the little Screech Owl are red to this day. Then the Hooting Owl and Horned Owl went, as they were proud as well of their good vision.

But by the time they got to the hollow tree, the fire was burning so fiercely that the smoke nearly blinded them, and the ashes carried up by the wind made white rings around their eyes. They had to come home without fire. And for all their rubbing, they were never able to get rid of all the white rings. Now no more of the birds would dare to approach the tree. So the little colorful snake, now called Black Racer, said he would go through the water and bring back some fire. He swam across to the island and crawled through the grass to the tree and went into a small hole at the bottom.

The smoke and heat were too much for him, too. After dodging about blindly over the hot ashes until he was almost on fire, he managed by good luck to get out again at the same hole. But his body had been scorched black. And he has ever since had the habit of darting and doubling back on his track as if trying to escape close quarters or rearing back from intense heat. He came back and the great black snake, Climber, offered to go for the fire. He swam over to the island, climbed up the tree on the outside as the black snake always does. But when he put his head down into the tree, the smoke choked him and he fell into the burning stump. Before he could climb out, he was a black as little Black-Racer. Now the animals held another council, for there was still no fire and the world was still cold. But birds, snakes, and four-footed animals all had some excuse for not going. They were all afraid to venture near the burning sycamore tree.

The water spider at last said that she would go. She was not the water spider that looks like a mosquito, but the other one with black downy hair and red stripes on her body. She can run on top of the water or dive to the bottom. She would have no problem getting to the other island. But how could she bring back the fire?

"I'll manage that," said Spider Woman. Whereupon she spun a thread from her body and wove it into a bowl that she fastened to her back. Then she crossed to the island and went to through the grass to where the fire was still burning. She put one little coal of fire into her bowl and came back with it. Ever since we've had fire, Water Spider still has her bowl on her back to this day.

This is one of many stories passed down for hundreds of years. They are multilayered and have many hidden lessons, some of which can take years to come to light. Others can be interpreted almost immediately. Water Spider is the smallest and humblest of all the creatures. Grandmother Spider also represents the web of life, which shows how we are all related. If we realize what this means, we will be more compassionate to each other, as Grandmother Spider is. We never know who among us is going to find strength beyond themselves and become the hero, and who is going to run away. As we say, "you never know whom you are talking to."

In tribal society, all weaknesses become self-evident, and the stronger and larger members of the tribe can intimidate the lesser. That's why it is of utmost importance that everyone feels needed and respected, even indispensable. Elders trying to help the small and weak to remain confident in "the system" can use stories like this as parables to bolster their confidence, and show that the weakest and humblest tribal member can turn out to be the most important. The spider is by far the smallest of the creatures mentioned.

Children especially appreciate that part. It is said in Cherokee, "treat every person, from the tiniest child to the eldest elder, with respect at all times." We also say, "each morning upon rising and each morning before sleeping, give thanks for the life within you and for all life, for good things Creator has given you, and for the opportunity to grow a little more each day."

The following Lakota song was composed back in the days when those above spoke directly with the ones here on Earth. It was composed before the day of the tom tom. That gives the fire song an interesting history, for we know that the tom tom is a very old instrument. It was sung lying on the back and beating on the chest to keep rhythm.

The Fire Song

by Lame Deer[26]

Wan Kata heya pe	from above someone said
Wan Kata heya pe	from above someone said
Wan Kata heya pe	from above someone said
Makata ile ile ye	that there is fire under the Earth
he eyape	
E ye yo.	

In order to be a holy man, one should find the visions there, in nature. According to Lame Deer (Lakota), as stated in his book,

"To the West a man has the power from the Buffalo.
From the North, he gets the power from the thunder beings.
From the East, his strength comes from the spirit horse and the elk.
From the Sky, he will receive the wisdom of the Great Eagle.
From beneath, from the Earth, he will receive the mother's food. "

This is the way to become wic'as'a' wakan, to learn the secret language, to speak about sacred things, to work with the stones and herbs, to use the pipe. ("wic'as'a' wakan is the term for a Lakota priest of the old religion; a medicine man is called pejuta wic'as'a.") Each of us has a special gift Grandfather has given us. We just have to find it and hone it. Use it for good, share it with others. The Creator had blessed me with the

ability of making art and making things with my hands, and for this I am grateful and give thanks every time I pray. Creator blesses me in so many ways. It makes my heart glad when these things can be used to put a smile on someone's face, be a blessing, or touch them in some way. It is priceless. These things were meant to be shared. They belong to the Creator and were shared with us out of love.
A lesson of what should be done with these gifts. You can only keep it if you give it to someone else.

Even though I am caged up, my spirit is free to fly with hawk and eagle. The spirit cannot be caged unless you allow it, and lose the true path. It is difficult.
Another lesson of the North beyond the Great Brown Mountains teaches us that the climb is high and very steep, but through perseverance and volition (or will), we can reach the top and soar.
Another lesson of the North is of the Sacred Lake, where we look into the reflection of the water and see ourselves for what and who we really are and accept it for what it is and plan for changes where needed.
These are two of the first lessons I have learned. Maybe they can be applied to your life. I have found many levels of truth in them, so it is good.

A good Brother shared with me a lesson that I will also share. If you come to a crossroads or point in your life and are unsure which path to take or an important decision to make, ask yourself, "does it grow corn"? In other words, "does it produce fruit?"

If we could all get back to being simple and get reconnected with Mother Earth and our relations, then perhaps we will see the Sacred Tree producing fruit, causing the Sacred Hoop and the nations to heal. We are destroying all of our wildlife, each other, polluting Father Sky, and slowly choking Earth Mother to death and destroying ourselves in the process.

We are all one. Without one, the rest will die also. If we learn to work together and protect these wonderful things, we can survive as a species. Maybe 2012 will be the year of enlightenment.

We've got to get back to the Indian way of thinking. If you have never heard of the Sacred Tree, you can find a little more information in *Black Elk Speaks* by John G. Neihardt. I pray each day for wisdom, understanding, humbleness, love, respect, balance, harmony, and the ability to try to stay focused on the Medicine Path. It is very difficult at times, but through prayer and belief, we can count on help from the Creator.

We are not alone, but we have to be true at heart and sincere. The pipe is not a toy. The herbs are not to be misused, especially the tobacco. It is the most sacred herb of our people. It is a gift from Grandfather, as are all the other herbs. It should not be abused or disrespected.
It is used for ceremonies, to send prayers. It represents the visible breath and the breath of life. These things can bring danger or harm if misused. It is not a game. Do not be fooled.

When being burned, tobacco is also everything in the universe sacrificing itself to the fire for Grandfather. If ceremonial tobacco is misused, it disrespects our ceremonies, the Great Spirit, our relations, elders, women, children, and warriors. They gave their lives and hid these teachings, ceremonies, languages and ways of life so that we could have what we have today. This is why those serious about this way of life, and who have not lost sight of the top of the mountain, are so protective of our ceremonies and Sacred Hoops (circles.) And those who have respect for the Great Spirit, they are remembering what it is really about.

We are all one. Let us again focus on the top of the mountain so we can climb together, and learn to soar with the eagles and protect what we have.

We are responsible for the next seven generations and more. Our responsibility is to learn these things and pass them on to our children and youth as a protective measure, and to assure that the sacred beliefs go untainted and live on. We owe it to our people and ancestors who gave so that we could live, and the Great Spirit who gave these things to us. We cannot allow it to die at any cost. It must be shared, passed down, respected, cherished, and held close to our hearts for generations to come.

> O Grandfather Great Spirit, we come together to send a voice as one.
> We give thanks for the spirit of the wind that stirs our spirits and sends messages to our hearts.
> We give thanks for the red way of life, for the sacred herbs and sacred fire.
> Protect our sacred hoops and keep them pure and strong.
> Teach us the way and give us focus on what is true and pure.
> Wah Doh! (I give thanks)

To each of my Brothers of the Buffalo: I owe you much, especially the teachers from whom I have learned along the way. Good brothers who made sure I never went hungry and never needed for anything. Never had to ask my Indian Brothers, who have offered a shoulder to lean on and always had an ear for my words. Brothers who showed me respect, love, understanding, and patience: you will always be close to my heart.

These then are the things that taught me the most about being Indian. They taught me the values of family and love. Important values which I lost sight of a long time ago, and which I've found again. My Brothers would never accept any compensation for these teachings. They were given freely from the heart. I will share these things with other brothers and sisters, passing them on as they were passed on to me, and keep to the traditional ways.

When I do these things, some people do not understand why, but in my heart I am remembering the Brothers who gave unselfishly from the heart. And my spirit feels good to help those in need, especially the ones who would never ask for it. They shouldn't even have to, we are all one. It is like the bundle of seven arrows. Alone, one can be broken, but together we are strong and unbreakable. This is the way of truth. "Mitakuye Oyasin" (all my relations).[27]

I want to be a teacher, learner, healer, and a protector of Mother Earth. I hope Grandfather continues to send me teachers to give me the right medicine. Grandfather has been working hard in my life answering my prayers, opening doors to opportunities, and ways to help my people. He is good to us. I sometimes get impatient wanting to do more, but I have to remind myself that we travel the Medicine Wheel on a white horse named Patience and I pray that the lessons be gentle. You know, we will always make mistakes, but it is only a mistake if we fail to learn from it and don't share the lesson with others. It is like seeking a vision.

We must make ourselves lower than the smallest creature, even lower than water on the ground, humbling ourselves, having good pure intentions, and asking Grandfather for help. Try to make ourselves as pure and clean as possible when seeking these things.

It may not happen the first time, but try again and again with respect, humbleness, and faith. Visions are very real. They are not myth or things of the past. They can be found if proper steps are taken. The Great Spirit loves to help us, but we have to be ready for what he has to offer and have the right intentions.

We have much to learn as a people.

One can only learn very little in a whole lifetime. I wish I had walked this path from youth, but this is not the case. Perhaps I was not ready yet. We have to start somewhere and work with what we have.

I am glad for the opportunity to share some of my life lessons. If it can only help or encourage just one person, it was worth it.

I give thanks to the ancestors, the warriors, the chiefs, the women and children who struggled, fought, died, and protected this way of life, the traditions and the ceremonies so that we can have these things today.

I give thanks to Astil-dihye-gi, the fire carriers and Atsi la-wa-I, the fire relative.
I thank every tribe of every nation on Turtle Island and across Mother Earth.
For all the brothers and sisters in the iron house, you are not forgotten.
All who are reaching out to help their people and protect this way of life, I give many thanks.
I give thanks and great respect to Wake Forest University for making this book happen and the great efforts for helping our hoops and preserve our traditions. Thank you!

The Blessing Way (Cherokee teachings for harmony and balance by Michael Tlanusta Garrett)

Oh Great One, I come before you in a humble manner,
Giving thanks for all living beings in creation.
I offer the clarity of my mind, body, spirit, and natural space as a prayer to You.

O Great One, to the spirit of all creation
I offer great thanks and what gifts I have
to the four sacred directions and powers of the universe.

And I pray
To the spirit of fire in the East,
To the spirit of earth in the South,
To the spirit of water in the West,
To the spirit of wind in the North

I pray and give thanks to you, O Great One.
I pray and give thanks to Mother Earth, Father Sky, Grandfather Sun, Grandmother Moon, and all the relations in the Greater Circle of Life
I thank you for your power, energy, wisdom, and sacred gifts, because without you and guidance of all my relations, I would not be able to live, love, grow, feel,

and learn.
I ask that I be shown another way if I have ever harmed or hurt other living things.
I pray by offering what gifts I have that you may guide us, heal us, purify us, and protect us.
I pray for all our relations that we may exist together in harmony and balance. "Wah Doh!"

To all my relations (Mitakuye Oyasin),

Snow Hawk

CHANGE

Red Horse

Change is the stages of a boy into a man, girl into woman,
young into old and sadness to happiness…
Change is days and nights, rain into snow,
It's also within the heart and soul…
Change can come and change can go like the wind from East to West as it blows…
Change is something we all go through, but the Creator's unchanging love is the
greatest gift of all.

MY WALK

Carl Smiling Wolf

Born in Monterey, California on September 26, 1980, I grew up a few hours from Monterey in San Diego right on the border of Mexico. I have six sisters and three brothers. I didn't grow up with all of them. The three oldest were gone before I can remember and four others were only there a short time. From what I was told, my father left us before I was born. Sometime after I was born, we moved to Daytona Beach, Florida where my mother lived with me and her soon to be husband, who adopted me and gave me his last name. He and my mother had three kids together. Their marriage didn't last long and he soon left us. He came back and took two kids while they were playing outside one day. Mom thought someone kidnapped them. She was devastated and called the Police, but they knew that their Dad took them. His brother was a Daytona Beach cop at the time. They told my Mom there was nothing she could do because he was their father.

My Mom tried to get them back, but with no luck. We finally moved back to California. My Mom met a man there whom she married. At first, he was alright, but after a while, I started to not like him. He would pay more attention to my sisters and left me out of a lot of things they did together. We moved to Guam from CA, the five of us: Mom, her husband, two siblings, and me. Where I went to Elementary School, I was teased a lot, because even though I am half Chamorro, I could not speak it nor did I really look it. Me and my sisters got to meet a lot of family and got to know a little of the culture. We stayed there for two years, '88 and '89, and moved back to California that year. I was nine years old. My older sister and I got enrolled in school there. The youngest was still too little to go. I never really liked going to school from the start. And not having enough money to get nice clothes made it even worse.

Somehow Mom got up some money and got me into baseball. I enjoyed playing and was actually good at it. We came in third place that season. Middle school wasn't so bad. I had two friends, Chris and Armando. We were best friends and did almost everything together. I don't really remember too many details from my childhood. I guess because it wasn't so great. But I don't blame my Mom for it.

High School is when I started to get into trouble. I went to Mount Miguel High in Spring Valley in San Diego. I didn't have many friends. As a matter of fact, I only had one. His name is Ricky, a short chunky Chicano. We tried to start our own gang. I hardly went to school and when I did, I never paid attention in class. Ricky and I would stroll around on the San Diego trolley till school was out. We would steal liquor from the liquor store and get drunk. We would go to restaurants, the ones where you would pay after you ate, and run out afterward. The employees would run out and start yelling at us. We laughed like crazy.

I met this girl back then named Trish. I thought I was in love with her. I would walk to her house almost every day to see her. Sometimes we would sneak out at night and go to parties and smoke weed and get drunk. She had this friend. I don't remember his name, but he was the only kid we knew who had a car.

One day we were riding down the street in Spring Valley and this kid was walking home from school. I was trying to impress them and said I was going to rob him and asked this friend to pull up on him. He did and I got out and told this kid to give me his book bag and money. The kid said he didn't have any. I thought he was lying, so I punched him in the face and took his book bag and wallet. The kid wasn't lying. He didn't have any money. There wasn't even anything in his bag worth something. That same week, I went with my Mom's husband helping him to deliver phone books. I remember his pager going off and him stopping to use the pay phone. When he came back, he said we had to go home. I thought something was wrong, but I didn't say anything. I don't notice the unmarked car on the road and when I open the door to the house, my Mom is sitting on the couch crying. I'm walking towards her and ask, "What's wrong?" when two detectives come from behind the door. Mom tells me she is sorry, but she had to do what she did. I hugged her and kissed my Mom good bye, and they took me to jail. Come to find out the kid I robbed got the plate number down.

My girlfriend's friend told on her and she told on me. They didn't go to jail. I got six months. I got sent to a place called Campo out in the mountains. They ran it like the army. I had to get up early in the morning and run and do physical training. That was the first time I did time.

I got out on probation and when I got home, my sister J. just had a baby. J. and I are real close, but we fight a lot. I don't know what started the argument that day. I think I was telling her how to raise her child. I said some mean things and cursed her out. J. ended up calling her boyfriend B., her baby's father. When he showed up, he had his homeboy with him and I thought they were going to jump me, so I got a knife and went to the backyard to wait for them. They came back there, and we started to argue. I pulled out the knife and told him to come on.

Nobody did anything, but by now someone had called the police. There were about eight of them. They came with their guns drawn and yelling for me to put the weapon down. I didn't put it down and we were kind of at a stand-still, when out of nowhere my Mom's husband tackled me and the cops wasted no time in following his move.

I got taken back to jail, waiting to see the judge. When I got into court, I wasn't expecting to see my Mom, but she was there crying. I felt bad and there was nothing I could do. The judge wanted to send me away, but my Mom talked him into sending me to live with my brother A. who was then living in Waycross GA.

At the airport, my Mom and sisters were crying. I felt so bad. We said our goodbyes and I was on my way. I stayed with my brother, his wife and two daughters. My brother tried to send me to school and I went for a little while, but I had it in my mind that I was through with it. So I stopped. A. was mad, but what could he do? I thought the world of my brother and looked up to him. He liked to fish and go hunting and showed me how to shoot. It's weird how things come to be, but the shotgun I was shooting then, I would end up using later on down the road. I thought A. was cool, but I started to miss my Mom and California.

I finally flew back to CA. I was so happy. We didn't stay in CA after I came back. We packed all of our things into a moving van and moved to Fayetteville NC, where my brother A. was now staying. By now I am about seventeen years old, and we have a place across the street from A. I was always over at his house getting drunk. Mom would come by and I would be so drunk I could barely stand. A. would get cursed out by my Mom because of me. If we weren't at his house, we were at strip clubs on Bragg Boulevard in Fayetteville. My uncles also stayed in Fayetteville. My Mom, my sister, and her husband moved to Nahunta, GA because he couldn't find work in NC. I didn't go with them. I stayed with A. He moved to this little neighborhood into a house when one day, we were grilling and I met Eva. She was walking to a friend's house when I stopped her and we talked for a while. She gave me her phone number. She lived right down the road and was still in school, going to Pine Forest. I still wasn't going to school. We would see each other almost every day. Eva eventually had two boys by me. We split up before the second boy was born. She moved to Michigan where she and her family were from. She and the boys are still living there. I hadn't heard from them in ten years until I got a letter from them in prison. Eva had a friend named Beth whom I started seeing before Eva and I split up. I moved in with her and her Mom. My brother comes by one day and tells me that Mom called and said the police took her husband to jail. He got like twenty years.

The Department of Social Services would not give custody back to Mom. We stayed and packed all of my Mom's stuff and moved her to stay with A. They found my little sister a home with a nice family. She still lives in Nahunta and has a daughter. Not long after Mom got to NC, she, A., and his family moved to Daytona Beach, FL. It wasn't long before Beth and I followed. While in Florida, I got arrested for assault and went to county jail for three months. I get out on probation, but violated a few weeks later. This time, I don't get arrested because I'm hiding from them. Beth gets pregnant with our first child. A. and I go fishing one night and on the way home, I get pulled over and get taken back to jail for my violation of probation and do three more months in jail.

About five months after I get out of jail, my daughter is born in Daytona Beach. I'm doing drugs real bad and get fired from my job. Things start going downhill. So Beth, my daughter, and I move back to NC to my uncle's house. While there, his wife's brother and family move in, too. Now my uncle has seven kids. His wife's brother has three, plus him and his wife. Then there's me, Beth, and my daughter. That's fourteen people in a three bedroom house. We were like sardines. I can't do it, so Beth calls her sister in Norman, OK and we end up moving down there. Beth, her sister, and I get a job at a nursing home. Beth's a Nursing Assistant, and I get hired as a floor tech. We all three save our money and get a two story townhouse not far from Oklahoma State University. We were doing well for a while, but like always, I start doing drugs and drinking again and I start spending all my money and Beth's. We get evicted from the townhouse.

Beth and I take our last check and move to San Diego, CA with my sister and her family. I get a job doing fire sprinklers with my brother in law. It was fun living with my sister again. We would go and eat and get drunk together, or stay home and get drunk and talk about when we were growing up.

My brother in law had a three-wheeler and we would go out and ride. We were on our way home from riding one day and stopped by a bar, drinking. Beth and my sister keep calling, telling us to come home. When we were done and driving home, me and my brother in law got into an accident. He was driving. I don't know how, but he lost control and went off the side of a little cliff. The truck flipped I don't know how many times. I didn't have my seat belt on and got ejected. All I remember is waking up on a helicopter going to the hospital. My brother in law got stitches in his hand. I was okay.

One of my Mom's friends from when we were smaller lived up the street and had two boys we grew up with. I started chilling with them at their house a lot. They had another brother who lived there, too. I didn't know him growing up, but started chilling with him. He was on meth real bad and I started doing it with him. I was up there at their house more than I was with my own family. Beth found out that I was doing meth. We would always argue about it. One day, I was snorting some in the garage and she walked in. She had a fed-up look on her face and said that she wanted to do some. She said that if she can't stop me from doing drugs, then she is going to do them with me. But she tricked me. When I gave her the bag, she dumped it out. I was mad as hell at her right then, but I realized that she was only trying to save me.

My friend's wife stopped by one day, while I was at his house to drop off their son, because they weren't together anymore. We started talking and then seeing each other. I started spending the nights at her house and doing more and more drugs. I eventually got fired from my job. Beth and I split up.

I moved in with the new woman and Beth moved to a friend's house. Beth was pregnant before we split up, but I didn't know. I was going over to where Beth lived to visit my daughter and to check up on Beth. My friend found out that I was with his wife and told everyone that when he got up with me, he was going to kill me. I wasn't scared. I was thinking he would have to catch me first.

Beth had our second child, a boy, in Chula Vista. I missed the birth by a whole day. Beth was mad as hell and I don't blame her. I was back and forth to see my daughter and son at Beth's friend's house where she stayed. Beth started acting funny when I would stop by. I would ask her what was wrong, but she would always say, nothing.

One day she must have gotten tired of me asking and told me that her friend's boyfriend would come home from work and show his private parts to her, or she would be washing dishes and he would come behind her and grab her by the hips and rub his private parts on her butt. When she told me this, I wanted to kill him. So I made her tell me the next time he was off. She did, and I came over with a steel pipe with the intent to beat him up. They lived upstairs in an apartment. He came out and we started arguing. At the same time, Beth was packing her things.

The dude went in to check what Beth was doing, when my daughter comes out and sees me. I started up the stairs to get her, and she was coming down when she fell down about ten steps and banged her head really bad. She had a knot a little smaller than a golf ball. I never heard a child scream and cry so loud. I felt so badly. Beth and my son came out with some bags and we just left. We went to my sister's house and explained what had happened. She let us stay the night. The next day, I went and got my things from my girlfriend's house. She was asking me what was going on and I told her that I was not coming back. She stated crying because of what I told her, that I was not coming back.

Beth and I had no money and we didn't want to stay in California anymore. My sister ended up buying us a bus ticket back to North Carolina, where we stayed with my brother A. He had moved back to North Carolina while we were in California. Beth got pregnant with our third child. She had him in Pinehurst. Staying with my brother didn't last long. I contacted my Mom, who was living in South Carolina with her boyfriend, and asked if we could stay with them. She said yes, and we went on our way down there. Her boyfriend drove eighteen-wheelers and my Mom rode with him, so they were never there. My aunt stayed at my Mom's, too. So it was the six of us. I started working, doing commercial plumbing. I was helping my Mom and her boyfriend pay bills, but like everywhere else we stayed, it wasn't long before I started doing drugs again. I started staying out late and missing work. Beth would always stay on my case. One night we get a call. Beth answers it and it's my Mom crying. She tells Beth that her boyfriend had a heart attack. It was about five in the morning and they were stopping for coffee. When they got there, he put the truck in park, and it happened. Mom called 911, but it was too late. He died before they got there. Mom had to fly back to South Carolina, because it happened in Ohio. When she got to the house, she was a wreck. We all gave her a hug and tried to comfort her. Her boyfriend was taken to Florida to his family where he was buried. I lost my job soon after and we moved back to North Carolina with my Mom.

We got a place out in Cameron and I started working again. We stayed there a while and things started looking good. It soon ended. I got laid off. Mom moved out because of all the arguing Beth and I were doing. We got kicked out of that place and went and stayed with some friends of mine. I looked for work, but with no luck. I got into a fight with the guy we were staying with, and we left for a motel first in Spring Lake, then to another one in Fayetteville. Beth got a job at a strip club waiting tables while I stayed at the motel watching the kids. One day, when Beth left for work, my son wakes up and sees her leave. It was early in the morning, and the other kids and I were still sleeping. My son unlocked the motel door and walked out. This motel we were staying at is right on Bragg Boulevard and the traffic is really heavy. He ended up walking down the sidewalk of Bragg Boulevard. There's another motel on the opposite side of the road. The manager sees him and runs across the street and takes him inside, where he called the police. I don't know how, but the police came right to our room door, which was still wide open. The police woke me up and asked me if I had a son missing and to describe him. I said yes and told the officer what he looked like. He said they had him across the street and that he would take me over there.

He called another officer to watch the kids and we started across the road. There was a news van across the road that I didn't pay any attention to. When I got over there, my son ran to me and wouldn't let go of my neck. I signed some papers and started out the front door of the motel office. When I got outside, there was a camera in my face. Apparently the news van was there because of my son. I hid my son's face and made it back to my room. Later that day, the news people came knocking on the door, but I didn't answer it. I guess they wanted to ask me questions about what happened.

The next day I'm watching the news, and there is me and my son coming out of the motel office and going across the street. The manager of the motel we were staying at had seen the news, too, and told us that same day that we had to leave. We went across the street to the other motel.

I don't know what started the argument, but one day, Beth and I were yelling and throwing things around and someone called the police on us. They thought I was hitting Beth, because they asked her to step outside and were asking her questions. When they were finished, they came in and looked around the room and left. The next day, Beth was off and we were both watching cartoons with the kids, when there was a knock on the door. I went to answer it and there was a cop and what I thought was a detective. Come to find out it was a Department of Social Services worker telling us that he was there to take our kids from us. I told him that he wasn't taking anybody. The cop said he was going to arrest me and to let the man do his job, plus it will look better when we go in front of the judge to get the kids back. For some reason, my daughter must have felt the tension, because when Beth started to get them close together, she started crying, which made the other kids cry also. Beth and I tried to be strong and hold back our tears, but couldn't, which only made it worse. I will never forget that day.

I watched them take my kids away until the car was out of sight. After they were gone, Beth and I sat there in a daze. The next day we got all the information we needed and a couple of weeks later, we started the process of trying to get our kids back. We went and saw them every week, which was the hardest thing ever. Beth was pregnant the whole time before this happened. She gave birth to my youngest son after the kids were taken. The Department of Social Services came to the hospital and told us they were going to take him, too.

By this time, I thought I couldn't take no more but I had to be strong for Beth. We eventually moved in with Beth's Mom. About two months later, the judge gave us our kids back, but said we had to get jobs and go to parenting classes and get our own place. We didn't have a car and Beth's Mom wasn't helping us. We filed my income tax and got about $ 2,500. Because it wasn't enough for a car and a place of our own, we thought that if we left the state, they wouldn't mess with us anymore. We moved back to Beth's sister's house in Oklahoma.

We were only there for a week when cops showed up at her sister's house and took our kids. They flew them back to North Carolina and into Department of Social Services custody. Beth and I followed. Beth went to her Mom's house and I went to my uncle's. We started the process all over again trying to get our kids back. They told Beth that if she didn't leave me, they were going to keep the kids. She never left me, but told them that she would.

My cousin JR, my uncle's son, had just started a carpet cleaning business. I started working with him. I couldn't see the kids, so I started drinking real bad. One day, my uncle invited my brother A. over to barbeque. My cousin Bill was there, too. We were having a good time drinking, eating, and shooting pool. Toward the end of the night, A. wanted me to come to his house to drink some more, so Beth, Bill, and I went over to his house. When we got there, A. and I had a few beers and we were talking outside with Bill. We were talking about this dude right down the road that about a year ago I had some words with.

I thought he and Beth were seeing each other and I said I wanted to confront him. I told A. to bring his shotgun just in case something happened. Plus, I knew that some of his family stayed close by and that they were crazy. When A., Bill, and I got there, the dude was standing on the porch of his trailer. I had been drinking all day and was drunk as can be. When I get out of the car, I have the shotgun with me. I walk up to him and start asking him what went on between him and BetWe start arguing. I shoot him twice at close range. We leave and go back to A's house. Beth and A's wife know something is wrong. A. tells them that I shot someone and that he thinks I killed him. Beth gives me this look I won't ever forget. A. calls our uncle F. and tells him. He comes over and tells Bill to wait at his house. The rest of us sit down and talk about what happens, then my uncle leaves. Beth and I stay the night at A's.

The next morning, my uncle calls and says to come get my stuff and that I couldn't stay at his house. He also says he called the Sheriff and told them what I did and I should call them. I don't right then. I tell A. to drive me down to my uncle's to get my things. We do and from there we stop at my Grandma's house to pick up some money she was holding for me. I think about going on the run, but don't know where to go. By now, my Grandma knows what's going on. She is crying and asks me why. I don't know what to say. She tells me to go, because she doesn't want to get into any trouble. I feel so bad to have to leave her like that. That was the last time I have seen my Grandma. She died last year while I was at Central Prison in the hole. She is my heart. From there we went to Beth's Mom's to drop her off. By now I made my choice to turn myself in. Beth and I say our good byes. We go back to A's house and call the Sheriff and they tell us to come down. I tell them what happened and they charge me with first degree murder and let A. and Bill go. It really doesn't hit me what's going on until I talk to my lawyer. He tells me the State wants to give me the death penalty. I go back to my cell, feeling that all hope is lost. My family comes to visit and also Beth. She only comes a few times and the last time she does, she tells me she's leaving me.

So much is going on that when she says this, I lose it back in the block and get into a fight. I won't let the cell officers take me to the hole so they taze me, then spray me with maze, then drag me to a lockdown cell. While in the hole, I want to die. I give up and don't want to live anymore. I stop eating. This goes on for three days, when finally the guards tell me to pack all my things up. They were sending me to Central Prison.

I'm on state a year before I even get my time. The District Attorney offers me a plea for ten to thirteen years nine months, which I take. I get moved from prison to prison until I get to Caswell Correctional where I met some Indian brothers and start to learn their way. I was raised a Catholic my whole life, but I always felt something missing. When I started going to the Circle I felt whole. I'm not at that camp long, though. I ended up here at Alexander where I meet more Brothers.

My story isn't exciting like some, but it's mine. Where I'm at today, I am on my path to better understand the Creator. I want to thank the Creator for all He has done for me. My family, for always believing I could and would change and for sticking with me through this whole ordeal. To my kids whom I love and miss each and every day: Trent, Jadin, Savannah, Anthony, Nathan, and Nicholas. I am sorry for the pain that I caused you. I love you all. To my mother who never thought that her son could do wrong, you are always in my heart. Grandma, you are not here on Mother Earth anymore and I left you hurt, but I can say I think you would be proud of me now. I love you and I am waiting for the Creator to take me to be with you again.

WHAT THEY RATHER DO

Dedicated to Thunder Wolf

Little Bull

People don't understand us
They rather look, not think, and misjudge us.
They rather try to push us to the edge,
not realizing
they can't budge us.
They say only god can judge
I don't see how
when the courts give us a judge just to hang us
like a towel.
They rather throw us in prison and see us get slaughtered
than to see us in the world trying to provide for
our sons and daughters.
They rather see the economy down,
than to see us come up.
They rather lose a million dollars,
before they see us make a buck.
This is supposed to be the land of the free, but
they rather set a price and tell us we got to pay to live
But they fail to realize this is the land of the Natives
where our ancestors lived for thousands of years.
Blood, sweat, and tear's is what they shed for us
so blood, sweat, and tears is what we'll shed for the
next generations to come.
They rather see us fail, so we got to strive to succeed.
They already tried to take our land and culture, but
with the Creator in our hearts they couldn't take
our beliefs.
What they rather do is get rid of us all
but as long as our native hearts stay pure
then together we can stand strong.

PROBLEMS TO PEACE

Young Bison

I was born September 27, 1983 to my parents Linda R., and Tommy Y. My family was divided good and bad. Linda's side of the family was upscale. Those who made it lived in upscale homes, owned businesses, etc. Now my father was the complete opposite. He was a well-known gang member in California, but resided in St. Louis, Missouri, where I was born.

My first five years on earth was on ups of being a spoiled brat. My mother was incarcerated at this time of my life. I was being raised by my grandparents. My Dad stepped up and came and got me. I was given an option to stay or leave. Of course I went with my Dad. At five years of age, I was around nothing but gang members of different ages and different women every day. I met my grandmother about a year or so later. Seeing my first traditional Pow-wow, I was amazed. The years flew by.

I was nine when my mother came home. That was when she picked me up from grandmother's house in Lucedale, Mississippi. Brought me to North Carolina where she met my stepdad, who was a well-known drug dealer. They met during her incarceration in Kentucky. At ten, I was getting in to trouble for carrying kitchen knives around. One day, my cousin and I were walking together when he and a dude got into fighting. Being raised where I was from, you don't run, you make them run or bow down. My cousin took off running when a boy went to chase him. I stabbed him several times. He ran to his Mom. I was in the street, fighting. My aunt saved the little dude's life. Social Services stopped in after this incident to see if I was being raised right. I was only now just being introduced to my sisters and older cousin. My Mom was on parole at this time. I didn't know what was going on. She was getting pulled over. When the officer got to the side of the car, she pulled a thirty-two caliber, let off two shots and pulled off. I got dropped off at my stepdad's house. He was like an idol to me. Mom got locked back up, so I was influenced by gangbangers, drug dealers, and a Mom who didn't take anything. That's what made me a live wire. I was now thirteen.

I got my first little taste of money and I got addicted. I remembered where my Mom stashed the gun she shot, and actually grazed the officer with. I was in the street, hard now, different. I didn't care about nothing but my reputation. I shot my best friend's brother up for having a BB gun war. Thinking that I had a BB gun I didn't know, I pulled the trigger. Blood went everywhere. The next night, I was back on the gang round, back to my Dad's mother's house. When I arrived, she took me to meet her Dad who was named Red Bison. He was a big old Indian from the Shawnee tribe. My grandmother was Shawnee and Croatan. He called me Young Bison because I was like another him, just in a future time.

After this meeting, I was now known as Young Bison. I felt that name was just right, young hard head. My Daddy came and got me. I went to my old stomping ground. My pop had guns all over the place, so I got one. Fourteen years old, wasn't scared of nothing and with a Daddy who was an og (leader) with the Bloods. I couldn't let the legacy stop at him. So I had seen this young guy who wasn't from my hood with bandanas tied all over his arms and head. I felt he was disrespecting my Daddy's hood and I came up to him like, "what's poppin?" Letting him respond, he said the wrong thing. I let him have three shots from a twenty-five, took his flags and went to my pop's house.

My Dad said, "Is this what you want?" I said, "Yeah." He put me on the plane to California. I met other members from my Daddy's set. I was a little nervous because of all these cats I didn't know, but I wasn't going let nobody do nothing to me. Waiting for my uncle Popcorn to come get me, I was picked up an hour or two later. I was asked again, "Is this what you want to do?" I was like, "Yeah, got to live up to my pop's image". I got to my uncle's house. I see pictures of my family I have never seen before. I then was told what had to be done to see if I was qualified to become Blood. Popcorn made a couple of phone calls. Two cars pulled up and came to pick me up. Two hours I was coached and told what I had to do.

I pulled up to a park where about four cats were sitting there. One had shot my cousin seven months before this. I hopped out the Cadillac, walked right up in. A dude asked him, did he know the way back to Imperial Boulevard in LA? When he walked away from the other dudes, I shot him two times in the stomach, then shot at his home boys while they were running. Fourteen years old, I was a time bomb. I was a threat to cats my age. I set an image to kids around my way. Every time they got into something, they would say, "My homie gone shoot you, so you better leave me alone".

After completing my mission, I drove back to my uncle's house to find several guys standing and sitting around on the porch. My uncle stepped forward and gave me a red bandana and a black one. When I was trying to put them in my pocket, somebody punched me from behind. I felt like I fell seeing stars. Everybody was on me, kicking me, stomping and beating me. I didn't know what was happening. I was crying for the first time in my life. Getting up slowly but surely, I was bleeding and busted everywhere I could I possibly be hurt. I asked who hit me first. It was the dude whom I was riding with in the Caddy. I pulled my gun and put it in his face. I pulled the trigger. It went click two times. It was empty. My uncle and the leader of the crew were watching. They split me and the dude apart. "I would have killed you, coward. You stole me from behind. You coward, I'll get you," I kept yelling as my aunt and them took me into the house. This was my first run-in with the law 'cause a neighbor called the cops. The guys I shot in the park gave the police a description of what happened and what we were driving. The same car was there when the police came. I beat the charge for no gun and no witnesses.

I was then sent back to Missouri. Meeting my Dad, he took me to see my Mom's family. I didn't even remember them. I noticed my grandmother looked just like an Indian princess. I walked in and spoke to her. We eat and talk. That's when I learned I was Occaneechi also. She used to tell me stories about how my ancestors made it possible for them to live like that. I didn't care then. I was in the streets. That was my life.

After my visit with my grandmother, my Dad and I were on the way to my homeboy's house to see what was up. When we got there, he was dead in the street. Shot seventeen times because he got robbed. I jumped out the car before it stopped completely. I ran to his side and held him. I asked who it was. It was some cats from up the street. I asked my pop to let me get my homie's face. I waited a week until I caught the person who did it. My victim was with his brother. My Dad was driving. I told him, "Slow down, give me your gun". I had a twelve shot 45. My first two shots missed, but the other six I shot hit their mark. Being nervous, my Dad put me back on a bus back to North Carolina. My homeboy's Mom came to get me. We had a long talk about what happened a few years back. Her nephew was paralyzed from the waist down. I apologized to her and her family.

I made that mistake, but it wasn't long before I was back at it. My stepdad gave me some dope and another gun. I was back at it. I came back home one day and my sister looked like she was hit with a Mack truck. I asked what had happened. She wouldn't tell me. My stepdad did. Her boyfriend had been hitting her. I went to their apartment. He was a dope dealer, too, but he wasn't a gun dealer like me. He came home from the block and he asked me who I was. I said, "What's good with you putting your hands on my sister?" My sister and pops were coming in the door as I was pulling my gun. I shot him once. The second bullet grazed my sister. I felt bad, so I left, thinking that I had shot and killed my sister. I started robbing, stealing. How could I go back home after what just happened? I ran until I got caught. That's when I called my grandmother. I told her I was in over my head. She said, “You chose your road, now walk it”. I was about sixteen, soon to be seventeen.

I was proud of all what I did then. I felt it was cool to hear people talking about me from everywhere I had been. I was taken downtown and questioned about the shooting. Later I was charged with attempted murder. I felt like what I had done to the boyfriend was right. Every time something needed to be done, I did it. I guess the judge felt the same way. I got a sentence of 692 months, sixty-two years in the state prison.

Once I got my time (my sentence), I felt like my life was over and that I was going to die in prison. So I went for it with gusto. My first week in prison, I was on some anti-police. If they told me something, I would swing on one of them. After doing this a couple times, I realized I didn’t have a winner. Every time I tried to go to war with them, I lost. Everybody just let me go, no one was there. I wanted to give up, but it just made me go harder. I felt like I was going to have to make ends meet with what I had, and that was time. I got introduced to a couple of Bloods or so-called Bloods. I didn’t like those dudes ‘cause they weren’t like me. So I did what my Dad would do, go at those dudes. I was in the hallway at Morganton High Rise. I didn’t have a blade or knife, but I did have a pencil sharpened. We walked onto the hallway by the school. I pulled my pencil out and stabbed the dude in the jaw. After my eight months in solitary confinement, I returned to population only to get the same thing happen to me. I got cut. I had to get sixty-two stitches.

In 2001, my Mom found out where I was. She started pounding me with lectures, like, “What happened to you?” We never argued, but we did have a lot to disagree on. Like me being a gang banger. She went bananas. We slowly grew tighter as the years went on. My Mom was very religious by now. I was starting to search for answers. Making my own decisions and walking around like I didn’t owe anybody anything: I was wrong. I still was caught up in gang banging, but I was soul searching. I found what I was looking for. I started to do research on my family history. I got completely lost in my heritage. But where do I start? My Mom was just coming back into my life now. I felt like a child is supposed to feel. My grandmother was now in my life, showing me the rope of my ancestors.

Just as soon as things were going good, here comes the pressure. In 2005, my Mom came to see me at visitation. First time I've seen her here and my grandparents were trying to get me back in court. After the lawyer had told my Mom what date I was to go to court, she came to see me. She let me know what was good with everything we were planning for my future. I won, but lost at the same time. I went to court, gave back fifty-three years on technicality. I came away with ten. I was grateful because I had my family. Then, in December of 2005, my Mom passed away.

So I started searching and digging for practices of tribal life. This was my new life. I found the answers that I was looking for. I found peace at last. I practiced with other tribal members, becoming knowledgeable at the same time about different tribes' ways of practice. This is what I was missing all my life. I met a lot of Brothers on this side behind the prison walls.

I used to contact my family about the Brothers I met and still meet from camp to camp. I felt like things were at the best they could be. I had everything behind these walls: weed, cigarettes, cell phones, and a crew I rolled with. The money started rolling and I got side-tracked from my purpose. Not caring about my priorities, I got a shock: my grandmother passed away. I was in shock. This was my home plum. I lost it. I gave up on life. I started to drift back into my old ways. First got a dude for asking me why I was crying. I hit him in the head with a master lock. Six months back down was what I started with. I made it one and a half years. I couldn't function. When I got out of the hole, I talked to my sister. Now my Dad was gone to prison for thirty-one years in federal custody. My grandmother's passing away was becoming the driving force of my life 'cause the route I was going to go, I was going to get all the time that got cut right back.

I started wilding out on everybody and everything, until I got one letter. It turned all my wrongs into rights. And I found what I was missing when *Black Elk Speaks* came in the mail the day after the letter about my grandmother's passing away arrived. It changed me with the first page I read. Before that, I questioned the Creator, "Why? As it is, every time something goes right, you take something close to me." I got my answer in my thoughts later on that night. I was putting other things before the Creator. I had to make a choice. It was one thing or the other. I got tired of losing, so I chose my heritage first. Now I found that all things of this world were put here by the Creator.

It's your word on your choices. Make it smooth or rough. I keep practicing and going at it hard, but sometimes I get a little side tracked. I catch myself really fast, because I can't lose anything else but myself. I was shipped to Alexander Correctional where I met the Buffalo Brothers. I was embraced and shown that troubles don't always last. Immediately, the Brothers of the prayer circle, which consists of many different tribes, showed me that there is still another sun rise, which I feel is a blessing. When I seem to go away or off the road, they are right there to steer me back on track.

If my story means anything to you, the reader, please, make a decision. Make the right one. The great Creator has a road set out for us. It has its benefits depending on how you approach it.

May your days be filled with blessings and your nights be swept into the hold of the bear to grow your strength. Aho.

LOVE

Red Horse

Love is a woman holding her newborn child for the first time.
Love is two people living together until death does them part.
Love is the brightness within a child's eyes.

Love is knowing that no matter what you've done you think is too bad, the Creator's love is strong enough to forgive.
'Cause his love is like a circle: around and around it goes.
"AHO"

LIVING NATIVE AMERICAN

Miclo

Before I was in my mother's womb, I was only a spirit roaming the earth, waiting to become a living being who will fulfill the Creator's will and be a part in life's circle. My identity was already made. It was only a matter of time before I came into existence in the flesh and started my own destiny in the web of all life. My existence in the universe is a major part of what makes life in general revolve.

I and all humankind are part of everything in existence that was created. At the very beginning, humankind was made from the Creator through the earth, then Mother Earth produced food for nourishment for the first man and woman and the animals that roamed the earth. The animals made an agreement with humankind to sacrifice their meat for us to eat. The web and circle of life then created a food chain that we still use today.

The hoop of life began when man and woman began to produce offspring, because humankind came from the Creator. Man and woman lived off the land. They nourished their offspring through the nutrients of creation. Then, as humankind grew in number, people evolved yet all were related and connected as kin to one another. In the hoop, if one thing was missing, then the other would not be. As all the young get old and perish, their bodies are devoured by the animals and the circle starts over. The land animals get pieces of us, then the birds of the air get us, and when they die, they fertilize the plants for us to eat again. That revolving circle is one of the Creator's master plans that have been going on through history. Human, plant, and animal are all connected someway, somehow, no matter how you look at it. Over the years, different looking people from different places started separating into groups and bands of different tribes, which created our own ways and the cultures of the present age. We had our own land and animals that we lived off. We were a loving people and we never stole from each other. Even when we went to war with each other, we frowned upon killing our enemy. Our ways of winning was to humiliate the enemy so they would have to live with themselves that way.

Our people were good people who learned to cherish every living and non-living thing on our earth. We knew that the Creator created everything and everyone. To us that means that respect and honor goes to all and everything. We hold everything in a sacred manner because we're all as one and we're all connected. The elders of the tribe are our only source of knowledge from our ancestors. Stories were told from grandparents to grandparents to us. They say history repeats itself, and we're living witnesses to it.

There are so many stories that were brought down from the beginning. They vary among different tribes and cultures. They are all similar in some aspects, but also differ in other ways. Some tribes honor different colors, different animals, and different ways of praying. Some even have the same way of doing things, but in a different way. The way of the elders is the wise way because they lived a full life and have overcome life's obstacles and struggles and they pass down their wisdom to the young.

Learning about your history, and family, and getting the facts of your genes today, you see what runs in your family: diabetes, alcohol addiction, etc. You try and overcome obstacles by being better prepared and on guard to detect early problems. There are several things that I have to watch for when I get older to keep me on point. Some of my people were unfortunate, though a lot of them passed away at an older age in life, and so they did live for a good while. I hope that I am one of the fortunate ones who have a chance to try and improve their lives, and be healthier than some of my ancestors. If I can live longer, I will have more time to bring people closer to our Creator. Life boils down to trying to get people closer to our Creator and have a relationship to our maker so that when we do go, we are going to a better place that is waiting for us.

From the beginning of time, our ancestors went through a lot and they tried to leave clues, such as drawings, of our past histories. People decipher these clues and come up with new knowledge. For example, the Mayan Indian's calendar shows an end to this time with a lot of scientific evidence. Hopefully, everything will be ok. The clues teach us about the old ways and what did and didn't happen. They tell us how relationships were dealt with. It all varies from culture to culture. I'm sorry that some people won't ever learn who they and their people are due to a lack of information.

Some don't even have knowledge of their real family due to adoption, and you might not ever figure out who they are. So I give thanks to all my relations and to the Creator for allowing me to learn who and where I'm from. It takes some research to figure it out, but if you use a little common sense, it won't be that bad. When you finish, you'll look at yourself differently, because then you'll know who you really are. Then and only then can you start to become and live the way your ancestors lived. Then you can feel who you are. You'll become someone different, not only living for yourself, but for your ancestors and for all your relations. You start to become a part of the history of your people. You will leave a legacy of your life in the due season of your people.

As the sun rises in the east every morning of our creation, the bald eagle flies up early in the morning to watch over us, and to catch our early morning prayers for the day. He roams the earth watching over all his relations to make sure his Creator's magic place is running well and moves in order towards his great plan. We all get up every day looking towards a better day and place, and we go to bed never forgetting our past troubles, but the wise man figures out that the Red Road is the better path to where everyone is going. For us, that's the path to a better life in the end, the life of our ancestors. That life lies in the west as the sun sets and there, souls are brought to their finest form. That's where we meet our maker and where we're going next in our journey. We will end up with all of our ancestors and relations. This is a time of new beginnings.

As we're getting there, a new journey is set before us each day that we take a breath. So we live trying to do better and to get better results out of life's circumstances. It takes a lot to actually put all things together and in good order in your life, and to try and to create order one step at a time. Actually, it takes a lot to even try and find meaning in everything that you encounter. Everything has meaning, even though sometimes we can't figure out some things. It just wasn't meant for us to know that at that time. The hard part is accepting the fact that sometimes we can't change life's circumstances and that we just have to accept it. That's why older people think they know a lot. Many of them have experienced what they now know. They have lived and learned, and we're just living and learning. We have to experience a lot by ourselves. So it is for us human beings.

It seems that back in the old days, there were places of harmony and love in our land. People came over and made war with us wanting our land. They knew that it wasn't right to take someone's land from them. Over the years, the fighting has quit, but the wounds will never be healed. We can only move forward with our lives and build our future for our children to come. Those are the most important choices: actions to keep our culture alive and kicking. We were proud once, but now we sit in humility. At the end of the Red Road, we will have overcome all and be again connected to our relations. We are all the same people, whole and also part of a whole plan. From Mother Earth we came, in Mother Earth we'll rest. This is our home where we can figure it all out. What is meant for us to know, in due time we'll know.

As a work of miracles, a generation of my people still was around for me to have come into existence.

Before I was in my mother's womb, the life of my genes already was Cherokee. The life of living as a Red Man was set before me. Growing up in my family, our ancestors' culture wasn't really lived or cherished. It was only talked about and half-remembered. Most of my great-grandmothers and fathers were already gone by my time of any understanding. When we were kids, we were trying to figure out who we really were, but we sometimes don't really figure it out until we get old and wise. For me, I grew up in a broken home with a loving mother and sister and family. We were always taken care of through our Creator. It might not have been the best, but it was what we needed and it was on time.

I grew up not knowing much about my heritage or background. I always felt a part missing in myself. I kept on the wrong path, and followed the wrong crowds for a very long time. Most in my family, especially on the male side, were alcoholics or addicts. In the Native community, we all have the same problems. So I followed a path that a lot of my people went down on. I was doing the same stuff that people have been doing for years. I hadn't been around too many Red Men growing up. I guess that's why I always felt odd in the non-Indian crowds that I would be in, always knowing that I was in the wrong place.

Through my teen years, I was in and out of institutions and steady on a wrong path, the path of destruction. In a way I'm lucky, because I might not have ever figured out otherwise who I really am. As I got older, I began to meet a few known Indians here and there. And not to my surprise, we had this connection, a connection of family of a sort. They were my people, no matter how I looked and analyzed it. We might even have been in the same community in the past and wouldn't have known it.

As I got older, I got into a pattern of getting into trouble. I knew I shouldn't have been going down that path. I knew it was going to take me to hit rock bottom before I could start over and figure out who I really was. Both my mother and father's side of the family had

Cherokee in them, so being Cherokee is part of my life.

I grew up wearing a mask of what and how I thought I wanted to be perceived by other people. So I lived a life like another person the whole time, but I always felt some kind of connection with plants and animals. There was a feeling like I belonged into nature, like it loved me and nurtured me and my family as well as my ancestors and my kids. It is true. Mother Earth has blessed and nurtured us through many past and present trials. We live off the animals and the land to survive. The Creator provides all of that for us and many others. We need to be grateful for them and everything in our creation because that's what the Red Road is all about. It's about making ourselves better with gratitude and living life for all our relations and for our Creator.

I've always been spiritual in a sense. I've always felt that a higher power saved me through a lot of bad times even when I was in the wrong. He let some things happen to me because that's how we learn and get closer to him. Even our biological fathers discipline us when we are wrong. The Creator saves us from immense danger, but still punishes our wrongs. He watches over us and protects us and all our relations, all at one time. Being in tune with Him and Mother Earth is a goal for many Natives, because a connection like that is something very special in our eyes. A wise person can use the ability to communicate with the plants and decipher what they mean to you and your people's life. There are communications and signs to better your life and the lives closest to you.

Life has passed me by pretty fast. I really didn't get to experience a lot of life in my early years and all the life lessons outside in the world later on. Those lessons passed me by and the prison's lessons fell upon me. I have grown a lot in the past years, especially in the way of my people and Native culture. It's even better for me this way, because in prison, it's a mixture of cultures and ways of life. It offers a broader way of looking at Native Americans as a whole. After all, we were all created by the same Creator.

I grew up on my own, mostly ripping and running the streets trying to find my true identity. I could never find the true me, the person that my Creator wanted me to be. I was chasing the fast life, hoping to piece together my broken life. There weren't many Native Americans around me as I grew up that I knew of. And for some reason, I always ended up hanging out with a lot of Hispanics. We tended to connect really well. Well, come to find out they are my Native American brothers also. Most are Mayan, Azteca, etc.

So I now I realize that there has been a connection between us all along. Most of them had a rough life also due to their color, race, way of life, and the language they speak. The Eastern Band of Cherokee also has a different language to speak with and around English speaking people, yet we are looked at in the same way and manner as the Hispanics. This Euro-American way of segregation has been going on for a very long time. I didn't experience it to the extreme, because I didn't (back then) know my true identity, which would have led to a lot more of white pre-judging.

In school, I was pretty bright, making the A and B honor rolls. As I got older, I got in the loop of feeling being in poverty, due to the rest of the kids around me with so many new things and what not. I felt this way even though I had clothes on my back, food in my mouth, and a roof over my head as well as a family to love me.

When you say, history repeats itself, well, it does. As I grew up, we had to have help from the government, so it still felt like the old days when the English came over and said their government would provide for us if we'll surrender our land and things. To this day, the government still does this, but in a more sophisticated way. I felt a need for independence even if the results cost me my physical freedom. I was ready to get the things I wanted and defy the government's rules. It is weird, because it feels like a harsh feeling from my ancestors passed down through the non-physical element to still rebel against the white government that so much controls everyday life and the majority of our peoples living here on the land that the Creator put us on. Natives were here first and had good times with plenty of food and water and land. We loved each other and didn't commit many crimes. We were of a good loving and moral character, but as times progressed and our own bloodline thinned, we became a minority. What was once ours and given to us by our Creator was taken, and we were left with little patches of land to have to stay on.

I feel that in life, it was passed on down through our hearts to still want to fight against the whites to help and regain our independence. Although we couldn't ever regain what once was, we're steadily trying to expand and reach out to the brothers and sisters who are lost in the struggle. That's what it's all about. We're here to help and love people as well as teach our youth our past ways and how to live a better life than we have. We'll teach our old ways as well as new ways so they can progress and move forward beyond the obstacles we've already been through and learned about.

The love my family has is a love of Native people, although I didn't see or figure out this truth until now. I spent most of my juvenile life in and out of institutions to still come home to a loving family with open arms. All the signs and vibes of nature were coming at me then. I wasn't one with myself or my ancestors' ways, so all the signs that were coming, I never deciphered them. I was in a wilderness camp for a year when I was twelve years old. I loved the scenery and felt a connection to all of Mother Earth and the animals of the wild. I knew there was something special about Mother Nature, but not knowing my ancestral ways was as a blinding veil over my eyes. I kept going through life living a way that degraded myself and family. I followed no rules and kept living as if I were completely free and running with the buffalos.

I went through woman after woman trying to fill a void in my heart, but it was fake love because I was presenting a false person to them to love. When my true self started to show, they and I both realized that the person she initially loved wasn't really him, so in the end it really didn't turn out well. Over and over again, this happened and I'm just now starting to realize this.

There are so many people out there that have some Indian blood in them down the line somewhere. I knew I had some in me, I just didn't realize that it would impact my life like it has. I was breezing through life without a care or a cause. I was raised in a Christian family when I was young. We stopped going to church and even acknowledging the Creator when I was little. So a religious background began to be far from me and became distant in my existence. It led me down the wrong road.

The path of destruction was where I was heading. My mother kept saying, "Son, you're going to have to hit rock bottom before you get on top." She was right. I hit rock bottom, as I thought then, after my eighteenth birthday. I got incarcerated for a year. I did my time, still not getting in touch with my ancestors' ways, but I was trying to get my mind right and ready for a new start upon my release. As I got out, I did well for a while. I got married, but I also got back into the party scene and started messing up, committing crimes of all sorts. I ended up landing a long stretch of my life on a long journey, about seven and a half years long if I was good, but nine years if I kept messing up. It was hard on my family and me as a nineteen year old boy who had spent most of his life going through the same thing over and over again.

As I sat in the county jail, it really didn't hit me, all of the time that I was in there waiting to get my time. I was so busy trying to keep relationships going with my wife and friends and family. Although I was facing all this time, I was more worried about who was going to be there for me when I'm doing it. My family and a friend came to see me several times. When I caught my time, I knew it was over for me and any socializing in the world. I knew all the people that knew me or were involved in my life in any way were going to move on with their life and forget about me.

And that's basically what happened. Only a few of my family have still been around. I told all of them to go on with their lives, but in my heart I didn't mean it, I really wanted them to be there with me every step of the way. Every time one of them went their own way, I became more depressed and lonely, more wrapped into a box or shell around my own self, building a black shell around my heart. Each time someone left, it made it worse for the next person to get close to me due to the fear of him or her leaving me high and dry all by myself. Over the years, even solid relationships with distant relatives began to get thin as to corresponding and supporting me through the rough times.

I thought my existence was getting dim in the view of everyone whom I loved and who I thought loved me. My mother and sister and father were the only ones who were really there for me. They have been there no matter what has happened. My father was in the process of getting on my visitation list to come and see me, but then he ended up in the hospital for a knee replacement. I thought nothing of it, just a new knee for Dad. Then things went sour and I lost my Dad in 2006.

That was my breaking point, because I realized that my people are getting older and are not going to be here forever. Most of my life, I put them through a lot of drama and I didn't make them proud of me like I should have. I regret that I could have made my pops proud before he passed and didn't. I knew I needed direction, I knew I needed people around me who were caring and people of my own: the same bloodline as mine or like it, and people on the Red Road of healing and strength. This is when I started to try to walk the circle my ancestors once did. I found this walk in 2006.

I went to my first circle to observe in respect what I'd soon find peace in. As soon as I walked up and saw the circle, I felt the vibe of the circle and the people in it. I sat outside and watched as they smoked the sacred pipe and I prayed and meditated as they sent the smoke up in the sky. Everything was done in a clockwise manner. I didn't know the meaning of any of it. As I came back, I started to learn what the East meant to our people and the animals in the East and what it meant. Then I learned what the South meant as well as the animals of the South and their meanings. Then I learned the West's meaning and what its animals meant. Then I learned that the North was really special, that that's where the sacred pipe came from, and the White Buffalo Calf Woman. I learned how to pray in the sacred manner and how it's supposed to be done. I learned what the herbs meant to us and the feathers. There's so much to it, it's like another way of life. I call it a way of life on the path of the Red Road. The love of the Buffalo Brothers was so great. I felt welcomed and I felt like I belonged and had a purpose there. They were willing to teach me everything they knew about it. From camp to camp, as I went from circle to circle, I realized that most circles are taught and run the Lakota way. As I've progressed in my walk, I've realized that I don't have to pray the same way or honor the same animals as the Lakota do. My people are from the Eastern Band of Cherokee and their colors and meanings differ from the Lakota ways. There are some similarities, but it's just that different tribes do different things in different ways. So I started wanting to learn and put in the process to learn about my background and culture. As I began to do that, I started to feel more connected to the circle and more connected to the different animals. I started honoring the different colors and meanings, which in the end helped me to have more of a connection to my own Red Road. It was more beneficial. Now I have a solid connection to my surroundings and things in life that I once didn't have.

The Brothers that I've met over these past six years have come in all shapes and sizes and all types of caliber of different races. We incarcerated are all we have and for someone like me, the Buffalo Brothers are a new beginning. I am now finally surrounded with people of my own blood line. I wasn't ever around any of my kind out in the world, so the level of connectedness that I feel now is unspeakable to the rational being. I'm a new

man, a new creature. Our Creator of everything has begun to mold me into a different person.
I've had some problems and issues over the past years due to the circle and just like a community on the reservation still does, we've dealt with them and have moved on. As we've done that, we've all grown toward a better understanding, one that our people once had and knew. Over the past years, my family has been there and other people have come into my life to share what little I've had to offer, but that little bit counts a lot. We've learned ways from old war chiefs about strength and perseverance that affected our people then and now. I've met Sitting Bull's great grandson in here and it was an honor to meet and befriend someone close to his warrior bloodline. The people in the past are the reason for what we still have going on today. Thanks go to Leonard Peltier for working for all of the Buffalo Brothers locked up. He's the reason for the circles in prisons and I not only speak for myself but I speak for many. It has helped a lot of brothers to get on the right path of getting closer to our Creator. Some have fought over and over to protect our circle and to keep things sacred. My sight on the future stands large for our youths to grow up not like we had to, but in a better way where our cultural roots connect back with us and we begin to share the old but good ways. Prison has made it to where natural races are welcome to come together and be one and whole as one, and be brothers. We don't segregate each other. We offer our left hand to all of the Brothers who are serious in their walk of the Red Road. We as a people take the whole situation behind walls seriously. I'm proud to be a Buffalo Brother. I'll always be there for a helping hand for our Brothers in a time of need, just like my people of the past were. They were all there for each other and so should we. We're a loving people with kind hearts, but if provoked or threatened will do whatever it takes to keep our families, kids, and cultures safe. Aho.

SEE

Red Horse

See the birds flying in the breeze, the leaves
Blowing in the wind, do you see and smell
The sweetness of the flowers…
Have you ever stopped to watch the
Animals run and play as they live free…
Have you've ever felt the coolness of the rain on
A hot summer's day, have you seen the
Sun rise and fall into the depth of the sea…
The next time you see these things, know
That it's Creation that was for us to
SEE.

JOURNEY INTO RED HORSE

Red Horse

My name is Red Horse. This is a brief story of my life. I was born in Robeson County in 1972 to Attie L. and Lee Jr. H. They were never married, so I was born without having a Mom and Dad inside the same house, although I do remember my Dad and Mom spending time together along with myself, but only a few times as I can recall. I was young. Little did my parents know, I was born some would say a "special" child, meaning I was born with a tumor inside my head, at the back base of my brain. It wasn't until I believe four years of age until it was found, due to child play with my brother. He was born in 1975. We have the same Mom but different Dads, but to me, we were whole brothers instead of what people call half-brothers. As I said, the tumor was found due to our playing around at my grandmother's, where all of us – Mom, aunt, uncle, and brother - stayed in an old farmhouse, so it was big enough, I guess. I was a kid, what did I know. I never knew what being "poor" meant as a kid.

I guess everyone around us was "poor" then, because everyone lived the same. My brother and I were jumping on my grandmother's bed, and I hit the floor, landing on my head and causing it to swell. My Mom and everybody else just thought the swelling was due to me hitting my head on that hard floor, but my state of being was getting worse by the minute. This was all told to me by my family. I do remember, however, the jumping part -- that's all. Due to the swelling of the tumor my sight was gone, my walking was gone. I was even starting to lose the know-how to speak, all this within a few short hours of hitting my head. So my family takes me to the hospital at Lumberton. Those quacks said I was to be okay, just to watch me for twenty-four hours, then everything would be okay. Now I'm glad my grandmother knew better than that ("hogwash", meaning LIE). It wasn't until after we went to three different hospitals that my tumor was found. It was at Cape Fear Valley that it was found. By then I was almost dead. By X-ray they found that it had already grown into the size of a goose egg. Thank God for grandmothers. So they had to do surgery right then. Only there wasn't anyone inside the States who was capable of it. Here I was dying, and no one to help me. Talk about odds. So they kept the fluid off until they found someone who could open me up. Thankfully, they found that someone in England, a world class doctor specially trained for people like myself, so the hospital flew him over a.s.a.p. However, upon his arriving, he told my family that I had about a ninety-five percent chance to die, and about a five percent chance to live, the odds are still stacking against me, talk about luck.

Without surgery, I would die in the next day or two. At least by doing the surgery, there was that five percent chance, which wasn't much considering that only one out of ten kids made it through this. So it was a "damn if they do, damn for sure if they don't." Now that we knew the problem, there was another one before us: money. How would my family pay for everything? They were just poor Indians of Robeson County.

The hospital was in partnership with a group called March of Dimes. They heard of my case and agreed to pay for everything. I guess that was my first of many breaks in life. It took eleven and a half hours, a team of doctors, and months of recovery, but by the grace of the Creator and only Him I'm here writing this, and my grandmother, and March of Dimes. I never once recall my Dad visiting me inside that hospital room at all. I guess he had bigger things going on.

After leaving the hospital, I went to stay with my grandmother. Even my Mom left. I guess she had other plans that didn't or wouldn't allow her to have to take care of me, a "special" kid. It was for the best. Believe me, I had a wonderful childhood life, so I thought. Where I grew up, I was surrounded by nothing but family. My great grandparents had about seventy acres and it was all family there: cousins, aunts, uncles. We would almost fill the school bus up every morning and afternoon. That's how many of us kids there were. We all looked out for each other, plus our Moms and Dads had gone to the same schools over many, many years.

I went through a lot of treatments growing up. I have a scar on the back of my head that would never recover due to being cut there. I also to this day have a tube inside my head to allow fluids to stop from building up. It is not like it was when I was a kid, because then you could see it really well, now you have to feel for it. Needless to say, I stayed in trouble due to that, as did my cousins, one for all and all for one. I was always looked at as special by my family and friends, but nevertheless, I had a wonderful childhood surrounded by family.

The river ran through my great grandparents' land and over the years, it was kept clean of logs, weeds, etc. Sometimes there would be twenty-five to thirty-five family members there cooking, swimming, having a good time. Those were some of the best times of my life even to date. Being poor was never an issue, because I had my cousins, my grandmother, aunt, uncle inside the family that lived with me. My cousins were always around. My Mom came around every now and then as well as my Dad, like on birthdays, etc. I even stayed with my Dad a few times, but he was then married with a son. With her, I was less important. Never too much liked staying with my Mom, never really liked her boyfriends, and they didn't like me, 'cause no matter what they knew, my grandmother would be there. All I had to do was call. Everything was wonderful up until I turned twelve years old, that's when my world as I knew it got crazy. And I became someone else.

My mother, after twelve years, all at once decides she wants to be Mommy and takes me away from my life and throws me into one of loneliness, fear, drugs and her many different friends as she would call them, but I knew better. See, at the time I didn't know that my grandmother was getting a check for me, that's how I got my school clothes and things. So now my mother wants the money, not me, just the money, but I had to come with the money. By the way, my brother lived with his Dad, thank God, but my Mom also got him for the money. My brother went back at age thirteen. See, my Mom was doing drugs, so she needed the money and buy the drugs. Because of that, my brother and I were introduced to drugs. You name it, we saw it. We lived in a lot of places, went to a lot of different schools. Something I wasn't used to, so more troubles, a lot more, because I was the kid that looked funny with the scars to show.

I stayed with my Mom for the next three to four years. And during the time with her, I became bitter, hateful, etc. She never cared for what I done. In fact, at the age of thirteen, she gave me my first taste of cocaine. Now here was a lady giving her son cocaine that she knew had a brain tumor removed. Now "That was Love". By the age of fifteen, I had enough, so I came back to live with my grandmother, but things were never the same again. In the short time away, I had become one screwed up teenager, smoking weed, drinking, having sex, all what I saw living with my Mom. My brain had trouble handling it all, and the drugs didn't help.

By now I had that "I do as I please" thing going on, 'cause that's how I was living with my Mom. But that wasn't happening with my grandmother. So I went to live with different friends. I went to prison at age seventeen for stealing. I stayed there about eight months. Got out. I went to live with my friend and her family. Needless to say, her Mom was on drugs as well as her Mom's boyfriend and her sons. The cycle started all over again. At the time I wasn't thinking that I had a problem with drugs. I had done what was cool, so I thought. I went to clubs. I had sex without condoms; that's how my son came along. I met his Mom in jail during my many stays there. I never knew I was a Dad until years later. I'll explain that later. By now I was on the race to do all the cocaine I could, smoke all the weed I could, and drink the ABCs out of business. I tried to, anyway. All my money was for getting high. That's all that mattered at this point. Now I've truly become to hate myself. I tried killing myself, but my girlfriend's brother saved me and didn't allow me to sleep all night long. I tried again years later, but I guess the Creator saw something he liked.

I met this guy through a cousin of mine, he was working for him and I also went to work for him and eventually I moved to my boss's house. I even got off drugs for a while when I was staying with him and his family. In fact, he liked me so much that he offered me his company. He was planning something else. That was yet another break in life. I asked my girlfriend and she wanted me to come home because she was lonely. So I gave that up and came home to her because the sex was good. I stayed a while with my girlfriend, then called the guy back. By now he had started to work for his brother. He gave him the company. So I missed that chance to live free of the trap. However, I went back to work with the guy and his brother, then stayed away for a while again.

I got involved with my boss man's wife. He found out. I was staying at his Dad's house, me and my roommate, so they kicked me out. I lost my job. I had to call my family to come pick me up from where I was at. I found myself back living with my Mom, back into the drugs again. To my surprise, my ex-boss man's wife came to see me. Then she moved in with me into my Mom's house along with her boyfriend. I kept my drug use hidden from her for a long time by telling her I felt bad. She didn't know the difference, because she had never been around anything like that. I didn't even work for a long time. I let my girlfriend support me. I tried selling some weed, but smoked all the profit in cocaine. Eventually I did get a job at a local fast food. I had always been dealing with drugs if not doing drugs. Selling drugs to keep my habit up. Then I got a job at the processing plant, processing hogs. By this time I had gotten deeper into cocaine. I would leave work and go get the drug. The only thing that saved my job was that I was such a good worker. I would even leave my girlfriend there at work without a way home. I would stay out all night getting high, come home broke with no money, not even enough to buy a drink. I wasn't even helping paying the bills. She made it easy by doing it all. She really loved me, but I loved the drugs. I loved her, but my addiction was more important to me then. I began to abuse her. I would fight the law, get drunk and start trouble with everybody around. I had a "I don't care" line of thinking. I was hating the world by this point. I hated my family, myself, and everyone around. I only kept my friend around because she was paying the bills. I tried so hard to kick my habit, but I always went back because I found peace with that drug, a way to escape my fears, my life of all those years.

In 1996, I learned that I had a son by the girl I met in jail. By that time, my current lady was leaving me. She had enough of me, because I took her through it all. You name it, I took her through it. I took her to the point of almost no return. I'm glad that she got away from me. She later married some guy who also beat on her, but she would always call me. We became friends in the end. I always had trouble keeping a girlfriend. I'll never understand whether it had to do with more than my addiction. I think so. I met back up with my son's Mom. I married her, thinking I was doing right by my son, and I did right for a while. I was working, doing good, paying the bills, living a good life. I would call myself treating myself from doing good. But I never knew how to be a husband or father. I was even mistreating both of them to the point that I got our son removed out of the house by the Department of Social Services. In fact, we had to go to court and see doctors, go to parenting class and all that. It took about a year to get him back.

We tried living together again, but I fell once again into the drugs. So needless to say, it didn't work. I found myself alone again. I began to distance myself from people, stayed with a cousin, but my addiction would always win. I kept telling myself I wasn't hooked because I only used drugs on the weekends, but I started to use drugs anytime anyplace with anyone. I always kept myself up. I brushed my teeth, I washed every day, but I would go through the weekend without changing clothes. Most of the time, though, I stayed clean. I got into the church and stayed there a while. Everyone was starting to help me. I was feeling good about myself again. That lasted not too long. I was back smoking cocaine again. Now I'm just living day by day, in and out of the church. Family trying to tell me to stay in the church. I would try so hard, but I would always go back to the cocaine. I guess by me having that tumor and my Mom giving cocaine to me when I was thirteen years old, it must have done something to my brain somehow, because I couldn't kick the habit.

The thing I hate most is that I stole from my grandmother to get high. Everyone told her it was me, but she refused to believe that I would do that to her. I didn't even care whether I hurt her or any of my family. Like I said, I hated everybody and everything. I blamed my grandmother for letting my Mom take me. I felt she should have had fought for me, but they all were excuses, because I could have gotten serious help. Something I knew I could get. I even took my kid's and wife's food stamps, which left us without any food. My lights got cut out, the car's gone. I was left with nothing. I can't say it's not because the right people weren't put into place, because they were, all through my life.

I believe the reason I was lost was because I was lost within myself, not knowing who I was or where I had come from. Meaning, I knew I was Indian because I live inside the homeland of my tribe, the Lumbee, but I didn't know the true meaning of being Native. I was never taught by anyone. I only knew that I was Lumbee, which I knew because that's all that was around in school, town, etc. I went to Pow-wows, but never was that light turned on for me.

To this day, I can't believe I've lost so much to drugs. I did a lot of things because of drinking and drugging. I cut people, I beat people, I even once killed to get high. In 1999, I went to rob someone I knew who had a lot of money. I knew this person very well, so I knew he had money, and I needed it. I had just turned twenty-seven years old. For fourteen of that twenty-seven, I was doing drugs. I remember the night like yesterday.

I was getting high the night of Christmas Eve of '99. I had gotten my paycheck from my boss. I smoked all of that up but forty dollars, which I gave my son for Christmas. I smoked all my other money that night. I remember it was cold that night, but my mind was so high that I wasn't actually feeling the cold. I remember, as I was walking to the guy's house, I wanted to turn around, but my hungering addiction pushed me forward. I remember that the closer I got, the more my blood ran through my body like lightning. The moment I stepped on the porch, I knew there was no turning back.

As I was walking up the steps, I saw it play out before it even happened. It was like a picture show with only myself watching. As I kick the door in, everything became like a tunnel. I couldn't see anything but what was playing inside my mind. I do recall him asking me why I was there. I didn't say anything. I grabbed him, throwing him on the bed. I had picked up a brick outside the house. As we're fighting, I began to hit him with that brick. I recall telling him to shut up. I don't believe he was saying anything after the first hit, but within my mind I could hear him telling me to leave. I just kept beating him until he went limp from holding me. Even then I never knew that he was dead. I found the money. That's when I saw the blood on my hands and I saw what I had done. Even then, I wanted to get high to take what I had done away. So I left that house with the thought of," If he is dead, what will I do?" Then my addiction told me to get high with the money. So that's what I did. I smoked all that night and the next day. After I was through smoking, my mind allowed me to return to what I had done as I was walking home.

I had a feeling that he was dead. I had killed for drugs. Then and there my problem of drugs became very, very clear to me, but it was too late for that. The crime had been committed. A million thoughts ran through my mind. I thought of killing myself. I thought of killing any cop who came around, but instead I called my wife and son and they came over. I took a walk with my wife, which was unusual for me to do, but I didn't tell her anything. I did tell her that it may be my last time to see them.

As we were walking, this guy I know stopped and told me that the guy was dead and the people were saying that I had done it, and at that moment I think she knew I had done it. We walk back home. She tells me she loves me and tries not to cry. The cops came to talk to me. I agreed to talk to them, even had them believing I was nowhere around, even told them where I was supposed to have been. Which was at a friend's house whom I got high with that night. I stayed out about two weeks, I guess, before it all came out. The night they came back, I went with them.

I knew I wouldn't be back home and still haven't been to this day, but I will be in about five years. On Dec. 24, I killed that guy, and on Jan 10, 2000 I got locked up. That was twelve years ago. The night that I called home and told everyone what was going on, I cried, but I also felt at peace, if it was possible for that. That night, I thought first of the guy I had killed and his family, then my family, my son, my grandmother. Then I really hated myself for taking something like LIFE. That first morning in court, when the judge read the charges, I thought I was through living life as I would ever know it again, ever. I did a lot of self-searching as well as soul-searching. Eventually, I rejoined the church and I stayed there the whole five years I was at the Robeson Detention Center, or the last four anyway.

I was able to help a lot of people. In fact, I was always walking the halls. The guards would joke and ask me when I was getting my keys to open doors. I was going to school. I was talking to kids that volunteers would bring from schools, etc. All that happened while I was facing death row. Like I said, I felt at peace, but I was also very truly remorseful about taking that guy's life. They say all things happen for a reason. If that's true, I guess the reasoning behind all this is, I've become aware of myself. I'm clean of drugs at the current moment. I have to stay focused inside here, because cocaine gets in here more than on the outside, but my desire to use it has gone. The old self wants to show his face, if you will, sometimes, but I'm quick to remind him that he's been chained and shall never be loosed.

After about two and a half years in jail, I went to trial for first degree murder and robbery. I was facing life or death. My trial lasted about three weeks. The jury stayed out for a week deciding my fate. My lawyers did a really good job, both of them. I had a mistrial. They couldn't decide on anything. So I was returned back to jail, where I stayed about a year. I took a bond, but couldn't make it. They dropped my first degree charge down to second degree. They offered me a lot of pleas, but I never got any of them because they were too long, plus I had the feeling that something better was coming. I just had to wait and trust in God, and that I did.

I sat in jail a total of five years and two months. My second trial was getting ready to start, but the judge talked to the district attorney. He and my lawyers together, they came up with a plea of fourteen and eighteen years. My lawyers and I had a long talk together. One of them, she even cried with me. I believe that was when everything came out: all the pain, hate, everything. I stood before the court, admitted my guilt, and took my time.

My teacher at the jail cried all the next day, because she knew that I would someday be home instead of either of the first two choices I was facing. Also, the jail staff was pleased, because everyone kept telling me that I was a good person, that I just let drugs and street life take control of me and my own life. God had given me a way. By me sitting in jail those five years, it was counted as part of my fourteen years, so that left me with nine years to go.

I've been inside about five, got like four and a half and five to go. I'll be free and clean. I know this is just a beginning. I'll have to face that same world, that same life, but now I know how to deal with those things without drugs, because living inside prison will teach you to deal with a lot, especially everyday life. I've found myself on the inside. As stated before, I always knew what I was but never who I was, and staying in jail all those years set the ground work for my next page to turn.

I was sent to Central Prison for processing. There I would learn where I would be going to start my time. There I was, still helping people, but now I was giving guys hope inside God's word. It was like I was where I needed to be. Now ain't that funny. I came here from doing drugs, drinking, abusing women, and murder to end up helping people. I stayed there about a month before I was shipped to my new home. I remember that before I left, this guy that I had met gave me the "thumbs up" and smiled the biggest smile. Even now, all the inmates and guards asked me how I ended up inside here. But I was shipped to Lanesboro in Wadesboro N.C. I ran back up with a few guys that had come through the jail during my long term stay there. Needless to say, they were glad to see me as I was to see them, because I didn't want to be there not knowing anyone.

A lot of the guys asked me to come to the Native American Circle there. I didn't know anything about it, but the guys gave me some paper work. I went to my first meeting. Everyone was talking and seemed to be really enjoying themselves. We went outside to what the guys told me was the "Medicine Wheel", the sacred hoop of life. There they smoked the pipe in prayer, which I was totally blown away by. They told me that this is how our people prayed back when they were free on what I learned was "Mother Earth." So this guy saw that I wanted to know and learn more. He would talk to me, gave me books to read, and the more he taught me, the more burning the need became to learn of my people and their way. Our ways. The more I went to the circle, the more I learned. I was part of a family inside the "Sacred Hoop." I found love inside. I found more healing inside. I found myself inside that Medicine Wheel. The Creator was still placing things and people before me. Only difference now is, I've learned to accept those things and people. Inside the circle, I learned what it means to be part of something like Native American, the history, life, struggles, pain, and the good side also. I was myself within the hoop of life. I found balance there. I found pride. I learned the meaning of family, because we brothers are truly a family. No matter what camp, it's the same. All for one, and one for ALL: that's just how I grew up with my cousins back home.

Following the circle has helped me become the man that the Creator designed me to be: a strong Lumbee man. The circle has also helped me to deal with being locked up, how to deal with different people of backgrounds different from mine. Most of all, it allowed me to forgive myself and live a free man. Through the circle, I've come to enjoy the winds blowing on my face, the smell of rain, the birds flying, animals playing. Yes, I still have my bad days and good days, but when my bad days come now, I think of my people and the struggles they had back in the sixteen hundreds and seventeen hundreds and up to today. I find help from the four corners of Mother Earth. From the East, South, West and North, I draw strength to carry on. I've overcome things in life that I would have never overcome if it had not been the Creator's love that did so. I'm not perfect by a long shot. I still have my hang-ups, but I know that I have the balance to deal with those hang-ups with the teaching of the Sacred Hoop.

I now find myself being an inspiration to others who have trouble dealing with prison life. Now that amazes me, to be doing that when I was nothing but a man lost to himself within the darkness of the drug of cocaine. I've even received the Big Brothers Award of the circle at one camp. I'm so glad that these brothers took time to learn and show me the ways of old. Now I will take what I know outside and teach those on the outside the ways, especially the kids. They are our future. We must keep the ways alive. The only way that will happen is that we must share our knowledge with them.
I always thought it was too late for me, but now I know

that my life has just begun to show. Now I can go outside and live life as long as I follow the ways of the Sacred Hoop. No matter what, I'll make it outside this "Iron House" I've been living in for so long now. I can still see the old one, but he's chained up and far, far away from the new onc. The new one (me) is walking the Red Road, meaning the good path, instead of the Black Road, the road to death, hate, bitterness. That road is there, will always be there, but I choose to walk the "Red" one now in life.

I used to think that I was all alone, but now I know better than that. For I've got the spirits of great leaders like Red Cloud, Crazy Horse, Sitting Bull, Black Hawk, Red Jacket, Henry Berry Lowery. The list goes on and on. They are the true warriors for the fight and right to live free, free of bitterness and loneliness. Those are the spirits I now find strength in. The Creator has given me the chance to fly between both worlds in order to become also, some day, to be remembered as a great "Warrior" of old. I heard an old saying that goes, "a boat that sails backward will never see the sunrise." My life went backward for a long time, and now I am watching the rise of the sun as well as feeling it upon my face. And for that chance, I say "AHO" meaning AMEN to the chance to live my life over again. Not many people get to do so, and I plan on doing so in honor of the life I took. I want his spirit to look upon me and smile, because I've learned the true meaning of being called Native American.

May my life be of help to someone in need of strength!

NATIVE PRIDE

Red Horse

N: No matter what you think you know, an Indian stands tall and true.
A: Always willing to walk
with head held high.
T: To tell the young the ways of old, and teach the way of the Red Road
I: In times of sorrow we will look at times past for strength
V: Very much sure that when the time comes, we'll accept death without fear.
E: Every Indian Man, Woman and Child is sacred to the tribe.

P: Proud to be part of the blood line strong and true.
R: Respectful unto even the smallest of living life.
I: I will someday fly as the spirit of the Elders.
D: Devoted to the heart beat of Mother Earth.
E: Ending in death with the cry Hoka Hey.

THE ROAD TO BECOMING

Blue Hawk

I was born January 26, 1965 as Edward JC H., JR in Albany GA. My father and mother, whom I never saw till I was twelve years of age, were originally from Hillsborough, NC. Hillsborough is a little old historical town at the base of the Eno River on the Occaneechi Mountain. At the age of one year and nine months old, my two older sisters, my brother who is one year younger than me, and I were sent to live with our Grandma in Hillsborough. My Mom had taken sick and my father couldn't be found at the time. My Grandma Blandina had the four of us adopted into the family. My second cousin DIanne gladly accepted me as her son. She never lied to me about my real parents.

When I was about three years old, the spirits called out to me for the first time. I was sitting on a block wall watching the cars go by my house. My new Mom called my name. I got up and started to walk to the house to see what she wanted. I took about ten steps and heard the loudest bang. It was so loud, I jumped and screamed. A car had hit the wall head on, right where I was sitting. My Mom came running toward me yelling for me. I told her I was coming to see what she wanted. She asked what I meant. I told her, "I heard you calling. I was coming." She said, "Son, I didn't call you." I knew then it was something that she couldn't explain. She just told me it was God's angel warning me.

After that day, strange things started happening. All kind of animals would come up to me like they weren't scared. At the age of four and half, my adopted Dad found me sitting on the ground by the access door under the house. I was playing with three snakes, a black snake, a brown snake with a pink belly, and a green snake. I kept the three snakes under the house for about a week. Each day I would go out and open the door.

The snakes would come right up to me. My new Dad killed my snakes right in front of me.

As the years went by and I grew older, you couldn't keep me out of the woods. The woods were my peaceful place. My Grandma told me, it was the Native American blood in me that was calling out to me, the Occaneechi Band of the Saponi Nation.

I think I was ten or eleven when I first went up on the mountain. I had heard a lot of stories about this mountain as I grew up. The one that always caught my attention was the story of the black panther of Occaneechi Mountain. Many years ago, when my Grandma was a child, she lived on the Eno River at the base of the Occaneechi Mountain. The story was that during the night, the people of the mountain would awaken to the sound of the panther's cry. It was said that the panther sounded like a newborn baby when it cried out and that the mountain people would think it was one of their children crying in the night. For many years, the panther would roam about the mountain killing livestock, but never had a human been attacked. Some say the panther was the spirit of the mountain. Others say the cries were only the wind. Some even said that they had seen a huge black cat with a tail four feet long. Even today, if you sit outside at night on your porch, you can hear strange things coming from the mountain.

I myself have seen the spirit of that very cat, and it did have a four foot tail. A beautiful creature of nature. There is still the den that the panther lived in. There is a big bolder in front of the den. From the center of the rock runs a stream of the coldest water you ever had the honor to taste. I used this place as a place of peace and a sense of freedom amidst nature itself. At night, I've stood on top this mountain and looked out over the town in awe.

As I became a teenager, I still was drawn to the woods, but drugs clouded my mind and thoughts. Drugs took me down the wrong road for most of my adulthood. I have used women like toys. I would fight, steal, and murder a man. I went as far as to put drugs and firewater (alcohol) before my three sons. I was twenty one when my first son was born, whom I will call Jessie. He was born June 27, 1985. My second son, Clyde, was born May 7, 1987. I was with his mother one time. That was all it took, he was here. My third son was born December 5, 1992 by my first wife. His name is Jake, or Little Coyote. They know who their father is, but all the same, even as much as I love them, I neglected them as a father. Anyone can be a dad, but it takes a lot to be a father. I have a grandson and granddaughter I've never met.

Let's back up a few years. The first time I saw my real mother, she lay in a coffin. I was twelve at the time. It was a sight I will never forget. When I was twenty one, I got to know my real father. My mother's name is Virginia D. L., my father's name Edward JC H. Senior. Over the years, while all of this was going on in my life, I never once lost sight of nature. I remember one summer in 1996. I slept in a tent in the middle of the woods. I made eight hundred dollars a week and still stayed in the woods till the day before Christmas. Call me crazy if you like, but I never felt more free or connected to nature since the time I was a child.

The spirits came to me two more times as an adult. The first time, I was sitting on the couch with a friend watching TV. A black human shadow walked through the front door, stopped, and looked dead at us. It then walked down the hallway and through my adopted Mom's bedroom door. The next morning, my Mom's voice woke me up before work. While I was laying there trying to wake up, my Mom's voice said, "Edward, are you up yet?" I said, "No, Mama". Well, who just went into the bedroom? I sat straight up. I told my friend what I had seen that night. She went white right before my eyes. I sometimes wonder if it was my Mom's boyfriend of ten years. He died of a heart attack.

The second time, I believe it was the same spirit. It was the black human figure again. I was walking, and it followed me for two miles. It stayed the same distance at all times. Till this day, I believe that spirit was trying to warn me to stop doing the evil things I was doing. My sister Helen even saw a black figured spirit once. This one could have been our real mother's spirit. I do think it was someone whom we were both connected with at one point in our life.

I got married again in 2000. I feel that my second wife gave me no emotional support. My feelings didn't seem to matter to her. In 2001, my real father died. Even though I didn't grow up around him or had known him that well, I felt that I had lost a big part of myself.

In 2003, the worst thing in my life happened. I lost the woman who was Mom for me for thirty eight years. For six months, I didn't know where I was or who I was half of the time. As I said, my wife was no support for me. I worked three to four days a week and brought home eight to nine hundred dollars a week. She said I was a sorry excuse for a husband, because I didn't work a forty hour week job like a "normal" man. I didn't know how to tell her that I wasn't "normal". I can see spirits and heard one call my name once.

In 2004, on July 9, I was arrested for murder and robbery with a dangerous weapon. I won't go into details of the killing, because I don't remember them. I blacked out. I made myself a promise the day I was arrested. I've spent half my life getting high, so I'll spend the rest coming down. I hope that everyone who reads this will do the same. The first two years in prison I spent going over my past. I didn't like what I saw. It was enough to make a weak man go insane. The worst part was the frame of mind in which I had lived my life up till that point. Now I am at peace with myself thanks to the Brothers of the Buffalo.

January 30, 2007, I arrived at Harnett Correctional Institution: There I met two of the best people I've ever met. The two turned my life around. They inspired me to take my Native culture a step further and to "Walk the Red Road." Walk the Sacred Hoop with the Brothers of the Red Blood that were true to their culture. The "Native American Religion" as known by the public, but known by the true Red Man as a way of life. The way of life our ancestors lived many years ago, who fought and died to keep this way of life alive so that it could be passed on.

Being in the spirit as much as possible, I was reminded of my Grandma. I remember a poem I'd wrote for her. I entered the poem in a contest in New York. It was picked to be published in a book of the top fifty poems out of two thousand entries. It didn't win first prize, but the top fifty was good enough for me. The poem is titled "Grandmas".

Grandmas make wings for little boys to fly
Grandmas know what to say when little boys cry
I still remember her old weathered face
As she laid in her coffin of satin and lace.
I recall the time when I was a child
How warm it felt each time she'd smile.
I remember the days she'd take me to church.
If there's any good in me, she helped put it there.
Now years come and go. I am a man.
I look to heaven and try to understand.
I guess Jesus called her to sit by his side,
But he left me here on this earth with tears in my eyes.
'Cause Grandmas make wings for little boys to fly.
Grandmas know what to say when little boys cry.
I still remember her old weathered face
As she laid in her coffin of satin and lace.

I hope that this poem has touched you, the reader, in a special way, and that it may help you find your spirit to express your feelings toward others. All things are born, live, grow old, and die in the four stages of life. May yours be lived to the fullest.

This is my vision and how I received my Native name. I was on a vision quest to find my animal spirit and my

Native name. I prayed for weeks and days on, and I fasted for three days. The third day, I fell asleep and had a vision dream. I dreamt that I was standing looking at the woods. A blue hawk flew up above the tree line and dove back down like it was hunting. It did this three times. And the third time, I realized that I found what I was hunting for. I awoke from my dream as Blue Hawk. The hawk was my spirit animal guide.

My message to you, the reader, is to live each day with respect for others no matter their downfalls. Remember, everything is created by the Great Spirit in the spirit. Remember, all things have a spirit and can teach you. All you have to do is to see all things in the spirit. If not for the spirits, I would not have been able to write this for you. So I take this time to thank those spirits with a prayer of thanksgiving for all that exists.

Thank you, Creator, for the life that you give each day, and
For the spirit that guides me.
Thank you, Creator, for the spirit of the four winds,
East, South, West and North
Thank you, Creator, for Mother Earth who shelters and feeds me.
Thank you, Creator, for Father Sky that gives me the life-giving rain.
Thank you, Creator, for our four legged brothers, two legged brothers and sisters, winged brothers, plant brothers, tree brothers, rock brothers, all my relations and their guidance.
Aho.

Unless things change within the system, I'll be free of this place in 2019. In the meantime, I will continue to walk many circles and the Red Road with my Native Brothers. I have finally found peace in life. Each day, my ancestors call out to me to live that day in the spirit. I am thankful.

I would also like to thank my Brothers of the Buffalo, who had their doubts, but gave me a chance.
Thank you, my Buffalo Brothers.

PEACE

Red Horse

Peace is something that is found within the quietness of the moment.
Peace is finding the stillness of a summer wind blowing from the South.
Peace is watching the animals of creation play without worry or fright.
Peace is the falling rain of a storm without the thunder.
Peace is the smell of the sacred herbs burning inside the fire.
Peace is watching the eagle flying upon the sacred four winds.
Peace is also found listening to and hearing the sacred heart beat of Mother Earth.

But if true peace is to be found, one must look inside the heart and soul, and reach for the
Creator's love.

BECOMING LITTLE ELK

Ray Little Elk

My name is Ray. I'm a Lumbee Indian and I was raised in Robeson County all my life. I was born in Scotland County, because my Mamma said they took better care of you up there. My father's name is Frank Richard C. and my mother's name is Susie C. I got two sisters and two brothers. The girls' names are Shirley C. (she is the oldest) and Betty Ann C. (she is the third oldest). As for my brothers, one died of crib death when he was a newborn baby. May he rest in peace. Steven Lynn is the second oldest. I'm the baby. I was born February 13, 1982.

When I was about nine years old, my Daddy started to sell cocaine, because my Mamma wanted a nice house to stay in. At this time, we were renting a house. My Daddy always tried to make my Mamma happy. He started selling drugs and he was working. So one Friday night, the Law came to the house to see if they could find some stolen goods, but they were looking for drugs. I was sitting in the chair. The Law took me by the arm out of the chair and my Daddy told them not to touch me anymore. So they searched the house and they didn't find any drugs. Then they go to the outside to the cars and my Daddy's truck, but they search the two 1970 MACH 1 Mustangs first. Then they go to the truck. When they get to the truck, my Daddy pops the trunk of my Mamma's car, and they search the car. Then they leave. But when they leave, my Daddy goes to his truck and gets two ounces of cocaine from behind the seat. He told me, "This is what they were looking for." Then he took the cocaine to the woods and put it in the stash.

My Daddy was working with a man, his name was Roger B. They built houses in Fayetteville, NC, and when they would finish a house, the owner would give my Daddy the lumber that was left over. My Daddy was going to use this to start the house that my Mamma wanted. By this time, my Daddy had stopped selling cocaine and by now we got a trailer and moved right up the road from the house that he was renting in Shannon, NC. I have stayed in Shannon almost all my life.

Now that we had a trailer, my Daddy had started on the house of my Mamma's dreams. But that came to an end real fast. My Mamma and Daddy went to a party one night. One of my Daddy's friends told my Daddy that he had seen my Mamma dancing with a man, and that he was all over my Mamma and touching her butt. But it was all a lie. When my Mamma and Daddy got home, they both had a good buzz from the beer they had drunk at the party. My sisters and my brother and I were in the bed until I heard my Mamma screaming. My Daddy was beating my Mamma because of what my Daddy's friend had told my Daddy at the party. So when I go to Mamma and Daddy's bedroom, my Daddy tells me that I better get back to bed before he would beat my butt.

So I ran back to my brother's and my bedroom and get back in bed, because my brother was scared to go see what was going on. So I was always the brave one and plus, I was the baby. But the next day after the fight, Mamma takes me and my sisters and my brother and leaves my Daddy when he's at work.

So now we're staying in the city of Red Springs, NC. I hate the city and I love the country, because I can have my chicken and my dogs in the country. In the city, I get in fights with other kids of all races, mostly blacks and whites. We would be playing football, and my cousin and I would always win, so we would have to put the beat down on the blacks and whites, but then we would become friends again.

So now my brother and my sisters and I are staying with my Mamma at Grandma's house in the Mill Village in Red Springs. My oldest sister goes back to my Daddy's, because her boyfriend could not stay at Grandma's house. My Grandma did not play the shaking in her house. I did not like staying at Grandma's house.

She would have me and my sister doing all kinds of stuff like bring wood in for the night or cut wood. I hated doing this. We would go spend the weekends with my Daddy. I loved that, because I could do what I wanted at Daddy's house. I could even taste a beer every now and then, but nothing else until I get older. I am about ten now.

So we stayed with Grandma for about a year, and then my Mamma and Daddy get back together. I am so glad of this and that we don't have to stay with Grandma no more. My Daddy and Grandma did not get along too well. I remember one day, I was in my Daddy's shop on top of a stack of plywood playing with my cars. I saw my brother and cousin smoking a joint of weed. They were about seventeen and sixteen at the time, but they did not smoke all of it. They put half of it out and put it under a paint can with some matches. But they did not know that I was in the shop, too, and had seen where they had put their stash at. When they left the shop, I got down off the stack of plywood and went and got the joint and smoked it.

I was so high that when I went in the house, I could not do nothing but laugh at everything I'd seen and heard. My brother and cousin knew I had got the joint and told me they were going to tell Mamma and Daddy on me. But I knew they were telling a lie, because they would get into trouble, too. They never told on me.

We would have parties and my Daddy's friends and Mamma's friends would come over and they would bring their kids, too, sometimes, but not that one night. And they would play Roy C and Otis Redding, and my Mamma could get down to these songs. When she would dance, it would look like she was dancing on air. There was a man at the party and my Mamma was dancing. That man came up behind my Mamma and started to feel on my Mamma in a way he should have never touched her. My Daddy sees all this taking place. My brother and my cousin Randy J. and his brother James J. were there also. All of them were teens, but they were crazy at a young age. And all of them were my Aunt Veretta's boys. This is my Daddy's sister and all of them are Lumbee. They will cut anybody and that man was feeling on my Mamma. So he got a blade to the neck. They like to cut his throat. And then my brother came down the hallway of our trailer with two .38 Smith and Wesson guns. He was going to kill that man until I told him not to do it. My sister Betty Ann and I were crying, telling him not to do it. And then that man had to walk all the way to the store and call for help. The store was not that far away, but the way he was cut, I don't see how he made it without dying. But he did not die, he lived.

I have gotten older and my Mamma has left my Daddy again. They go to court to see who would get me and my sister Betty Ann. Mamma got us, but Daddy would keep us on the weekends. One weekend, I decided to never go back to Mamma's and Grandma. Like I said, I don't like the city. I love the country. I started hanging around my homeboys. We start smoking weed and partying at the age of fourteen. Now I got to where I don't want to go to school. I missed so many days that the Social Services Department came out to my house. They told my Daddy that I had not been going to school like I should. My Daddy beat my butt so hard that he cut the blood out of my back.

I was in school every day from then on out. I would always smoke me a blunt before I got on the bus. Then one of my cousins turned me on to Wu-Tangs, which is a crack-cocaine and weed mix. That was the worst thing I ever did. Now I am stealing from the people I love the most, friends and family. I was robbing these boys that I was fighting chickens with. Their names are Jamie and Todd. Todd sold big weight in weed. They would give me anything I ask for. But I did not want them to know I was smoking crack, so I would steal from them to get crack.

So one day, they had a big chicken fight in Rockingham, NC. Fred and Scott were going to ask me if I wanted to go. I told them that I was sick, but I was not. So when I thought they were gone, I went to Scott's and robbed him for seven and a half pounds of weed. I went straight to the crack house and sold the half pound for two 8-balls of crack. Then I started selling bags of weed around Shannon, NC, where I am staying with my Daddy. I gave my Daddy two thousand dollars to do whatever he wanted with it. I love my Daddy and he was my everything.

I hate the way I got on drugs. I wish I had all the money now that I spent in drugs. Now Todd has found out that I got his weed. My cousin who smoked all the drugs with me told on me. His name is Chad C. After we did all the drugs, he went and told Scott that he knew how he had got his weed. Scott is a kingpin and could have had me killed. He told me that the only reason he did not have me killed was because he knew my Daddy, and my Daddy was a good man. So he let me live, but that warning did not scare me. I went right back for a second time to hit Scott up, and this time I took my sister Shirley with me. We had to get on our hands and knees and crawl to get through the woods to the cock house where the weed was at.

When I was crawling beside one of the chicken pens, I heard a clicking noise. It was Scott's girlfriend standing over me with a nine millimeter gun pointed at my head. She asked me what I was doing and I told her I was looking for my dog that I had lost when I was hunting last night. She told me that I was lying, that she knew who I was, and what I was looking for. Then she called Fred, and then Fred called my Daddy. Fred came and picked me up from Scott's house in Hoke County, NC. Then my Daddy came and got me and told me to better stay away from down there at Scott's house before one of them kill me. So now I can't go to Fred's or Scott's no more.

I met this big chickening man named Allen who fights chickens. He had a race house. He would fight bull dogs. He was a drug dealer and he had money. So now I am going to stay with him, and I love going to Allen's on the weekends, because I had to be in school through the week. But sometimes I would skip school and go to Allen's house instead. So one weekend, Allen had to be in Virginia for a big chicken fight that he had entered in a five cock. I had to watch the house. But when Sunday came, I had to go home. When my Daddy came and got me, I took about eight cocks from Allen, and I got his good cocks, too. When my Daddy and I got home, we took the cocks out and put them in pens. My Daddy asked me, where did I get the cocks from. I told him Allen gave them to me, but I stole them from Allen. I sold one of the cocks to a man for a hundred dollars. I went and got me some crack so I could get high, and that is what I did.

So now Allen is back from the chicken fight and he won all five of the fights and won fifty thousand dollars. When he came to the house, he told me to walk and let's look at my chickening. And that's what we did. He saw the roosters I took from his house. He told me I could keep the cocks. I was so glad of that.

I was going to his house every weekend until the Feds got him on drug charges, and until we found out that my Daddy had cancer. This was the worst part of my life. My Daddy was a strong man. Then he got to where he could not eat his food. He was on all kinds of medication for the pain, but most of the time it did not help. I have seen my Daddy fight death three times one night. On the fourth time, we lost him, and that was on November 3, 2000 at the age of fifty-five years old.

When he died, I tried to kill myself, but my brother-in-law saved me. I wish he would have let me do it. I think I would have been better off, because when I lost my Daddy, I feel like I lost everything. I got on drugs harder than when I was on them before. I was breaking into people's houses, stealing guns, TVs, VCRs, and whatever else I could sell to get me a rock.

My Daddy had left me and my sister Shirley the trailer that we were staying in until the lights got turned off. My cousin Jason came by one day and told me that we could go stay with him and his wife Lisa O. in Hope Mills, NC. They had three kids together and my cousin Jason was selling drugs in Fayetteville, NC off 301 in the motels. He had about five girls working for him who walked the streets to get money to buy his crack from him. My cousin Jason knew I was smoking crack on weed until I hit a crack pipe. The worst thing I ever did in my life was hit the pipe. Now I'm doing anything to get crack. I did not have to steal to get it now because I was working for Jason in his drug house.

I was watching his brother Ra-Ra's back, making sure nobody would run up in the trap house and rob him. That's what I was there for. He is my cousin, too, and his name is Ralph L. The house that we are trapping out of is his girlfriend's Grandma's house and his girlfriend's name is T.T. She was getting high, too, but she did not get high around Ra-Ra. He would have beat her down. She used to walk the streets to get crack, too. To me, he tried to turn a ho into a housewife. She even tried to give me sex for crack, but I never did it.

One night, these two hoes beat three white boys out of their money and did not have sex with them. The two hoes thought that the three white boys did not see what house they went into, but they were wrong. The house they saw them go into was our trap house. Then the three white boys pull in front of the trap house and they start raising hell in front of it. That will bring the law around and we don't need that when we are selling drugs. Then one of the white boys said, "Let's go up in the house". I was right there at one of the windows of the house listening to the white boys with the windows up when they said this. So when they started coming up to the trap house, I started shooting at them with my .25 handgun. They ran and got in their truck and left. But when we went to re-up and get some more dope, the same white boys ran over the gate of the trap house and took it down.

Now the police are hot on us. We have to move to another trap house and so we do. We get hot there, too. We have so many cars coming in and out that the police is kicking in the door almost every night. But they never get anything because we are on point. We had to stay on point so that we would not get locked up. Now my cousin Jason tells me that he would like to have a trap house in Robeson County like he had in Fayetteville. I told him to get a place to stay, and I would get it jumping. So we got the place to stay from a black man.

His name was Craig. The place was a mess, so I had to start cleaning the yard and cut trees down. I told one girl that we had dope to sell. It was on from there on out. We were selling twenties on the up and sometimes I would not go to bed for three or four days. One time, my cousin Jason would try to lock me in a room and make me go to sleep, but I would go out the window. On the second try he got me, because he had bolted the window down and I had no choice but to go to sleep and that is what I did. But when I got up, I had an eight ball of crack waiting on me to get the day started, and I had a lot of work to do at this place.

One day, I'm in the yard doing some work and I had just took a hit of crack, and I heard something falling from the trees. When I looked up, it was a black snake and I don't like snakes. I'm scared of them, so I run to the house and I get a Ruger .22 rifle. I shot that snake ten times. I called my cousin Jason on his cell phone and told him to come get the snake or the yard would not get cleaned. He came and got the snake.

Well, now business has picked up and we are not selling twenties anymore, we are selling weight. Four and a half ounces to nine ounces, and I'm making all the twenties sell or 8-balls so I can have some money, too. I'm a smoker walking around with a forty caliber in my belt and an AR-15 in my hands like Scar Face. I had the best of clothes to wear, and I had my own house key to the house. My cousin could trust me. I was his right hand man, and I would die if someone tried to rob us.

Now we are getting to the part about why I am in prison. So we are getting money as always and one day, my cousin Jason had me drop some dope off to a man named J.B. He's a black man and he is moving about a half a brick every three days, so I want to go by myself, but this day, my cousin Jason wants our neighbor to ride me with. His name is James Ray. I always want to go by myself. That way, if the police stop me, I'm not going to tell on myself. I'm trying to tell him this, but he would not go for it. So I told James Ray to come on so we could go to J.B.'s, drop the half brick off, and get the money and that is about thirteen thousand dollars. On the way back to the house, my cousin stops us. Her name is Shelly. She wanted to hear that song by Fifty-Cent called "21 Questions", because she knows I'm a G-Unit fan. So I let her hear it, and then I told her and her girlfriends that we had to go.

We left from there and on the way home there were three state troopers. At the four-way crossing, we had to make a right to go home. James Ray was turning the radio and when he saw the state trooper, he leaned back without a seatbelt on. I had mine on, and when they see him do that, they come for us. So I told him to hold on and I punched that gas. They were on our tails and knew we were drug dealers. One of the state troopers' name is Trooper McCall and he did not like my cousin Jason.

When I turned on the dirt road and tried to jump out and run, they were already on me with their guns out and told me, "Don't move". I had a gun on me and two 8-balls of crack and half an ounce of weed and all that money. They got us out of the car, and put us in handcuffs, and put us in police cars. And what did James Ray do? He told them that the dope, money, and the gun were mine. If he would have taken the charge, he could have signed himself out of jail because he was under age at the time, or his Mama and Daddy could come get him out at the time. But he did not stick to the streets' code "DON'T SNITCH", so they took me to jail. I stayed overnight and made bond the next morning, and was glad of that.

So now I go home and do what I do every other day: smoke crack, watch the yard. That is what the yard dogs do, watch the yard, and make sure the police don't run in the trap house, and make sure nobody robs you. I was good at that and taking care of the chickens and my pit bull. His name was Red Man. I get on the four wheeler and I ride by James Ray's. He sees me and tries to stop me, so I act like I don't see him. I keep right on going and I ride all the way around the block and go back to Jason's.

I've got a homeboy named Shawn C. He and I are real close, like brothers. He's got a beef with Carl H., and both of them will bust their guns. Now that I hang out around Shawn, I get in their beef and so does Jason. So now it is a war between us and every time we see each other, we are shooting at each other. It doesn't matter where it is. So one night, we send Lisa and Shawn's girlfriend to get us something to eat. Carl and his homeboys start shooting at Lisa and Shawn's girlfriend. When they got back, Lisa ran in the house and told us what had happened. It was Carl and his homeboys that were shooting at them. So me, Shawn, and Johnny get our guns and we go looking for them. We go to all the spots where they hang out at. They're not at any of their spots. But before we leave the house, Jason tells Lisa to fix me about a gram of cocaine, so she did. I did some and we went looking for Carl and his homeboys. So we go to Thunder Valley, because at the time Carl is hanging around my cousin Willie C. But he was not at their house and we leave from there and go up town (Red Springs) to the car wash. We are sitting there and I'm doing the cocaine. Now, I'm ready for whatever.

I've got a SKS rifle and Shawn has got a 444 Marlin Rifle and Jason has got an AR-15 Colt. So we are sitting there and Shawn and Jason are talking to some boys that they call the Blue Brothers. They've got a beef with Carl, too. So we are about to go when one of the Blue Boys says, "Y'all can't go yet. There they go!" When I looked at the stop light, it was Carl sitting at the light. So when he saw it was us, he drove off. When he did, I jumped off the back of the truck and started shooting at his car, and Jason was letting that AR-15 sing, too. When Shawn shot that 444, everything at the car wash hit the dirt. I don't know if we hit the car Carl was in or not, but I know that the Police Station was about a block away.

I knew they were coming, so we jump in the truck and go back home. When we get there, somebody calls Jason's cell phone and tells us they had the car wash taped off with yellow tape, and that somebody had been killed. So we think we've killed Carl, but it was not him. It was somebody from the bottom that got hit. They were trying to say Jason did it. Now the police want to talk to Jason. His Daddy, Uncle John, got him to talk to them, but it was about something that had happened somewhere else.

So now my cousin Jason is doing some work to the trailer – the trap house. He is redoing the inside of the trailer, so my cousin Willie C. and his girlfriend are out there. He said he didn't want any beef with us over Carl. He and I are doing business with chickens and dogs. So I'm off to the side raking in the woods and smoking a Wu-tang. I look down the dirt road. I see a big white truck coming. I asked Jason if he ordered some new TV or chairs and he told me no, so I said, "Here comes the police." He ran in the house and threw the dope in the woods. When the truck turned the corner, they jumped out of the back of the truck and told everybody to get down. Everybody got down but me. I ran in the woods and watched them. One of them asked, "Where's little Ray at?" But nobody told on me. So I am going down the dirt road to the train tracks to make my getaway. But I hear a four wheeler coming, so I lay down beside a log. He rode right by me. Then he stops and says, "Hey, hey," and on the third "Hey", I jumped up and ran through the woods. When he tried to come after me, the four-wheeler cut off on him. So now I've got a good jump on him.

I go to James Ray's Daddy's house. They have a camper that James Ray's uncle is staying in. He smokes crack too, so we go in the camper and smoke the crack I've got, and that was about an 8-ball. So now the crack is gone and I want some more. I tell James Ray's uncle to go and see if the law is gone from Jason's. He does, and when he comes back, he tells me they are gone. So I go check for myself and when I look in the house, I see

Jason, and he is in cuffs and there are two police in the house with him. So he waves his hands and tells me to go on, so I go back to James Ray's house. But the whole time, there are police in the woods looking for me.

They could have gotten me, but there was a bigger fish to get and that was the man Jason was getting his dope from. He had called Jason's cell phone when the police were there. But the person he talked to was not Jason. It was the police. So when he asked if Jason wanted the same thing, the police said yes, and he told them he was on his way. The police were in the woods waiting on him to bring the dope. When he shows up, they get him with two bricks (two kilo). To me, Jason could have stopped all of this if he would have hollered that he was talking to the police when he called the cell phone.

When they lock everybody up, I take the car that the man had from whom Jason was getting his dope. I go sell the radio and the speakers and the rims to get me some dope, but I didn't take anything from Jason to get me some dope. I get me some dope and a chickening head and I do my thing. The next morning, Jason and Shawn make bond and get out. When Jason comes home, he asks me where the car is. So I tell him I sold it to get me some dope. And he gets real mad at me for that.

I go to jail on a dope charge and I stay in jail about four months. I call home one day and Jason asks me if I was ready to come home, and I told him, "Hell yes!" And he asks me, was I going to stay off crack and I told him yes, and I did so. I make bond, but when we are leaving the jailhouse, on Highway 74, I'm about to jump out of the truck. But he tells me that Jason is at the Fayetteville Motor Speedway waiting on me, so that is where I get out.

So Jason and his girlfriend Candace, his homeboy Dave and his girlfriend, and Nolan and I are at the racetrack. We see a black man who has a club in Fayetteville. Jason tells him that we will be there on Saturday night. He said we could get in VIP, so Jason asks us if we are ready to go home. We all said yes, so I ride with Nolan in the Mustang. We stop at Thunder Valley Store to get gas. Nolan and I are in the Mustang and he stops at the railroad and does a burn out and does something to the car. So we've got to cross the dirt road we stay on. When we got to the dirt road, Jason went and got the four wheeler to pull us home. But when Nolan and I were sitting there waiting on Jason to come pull us home, Nolan went under the seat and handed me a Glock 40-caliber made by Smith and Wesson and told me it was mine. I stay up all night long riding the four wheeler.

At daybreak, I go to Lisa (Jason's wife) and I wake her and the kids up. And they were happy to see me. And then Lisa calls my sister. Betty Ann and her kids come over to Martina's house to see me. My sister, Lisa, and I smoke a blunt of weed and then they play the song "Candy Shop" by Fifty Cent for me. I told them I had to get back to Jason, so I go back to Jason. Cam and Jason get up and we go and get me some new clothes and shoes and we come back. My cousin Ted L. comes to get some dope and asks me when did I get out of jail. I told him last night. Ted told Jason he had a SS Monte Carlo for sale and Jason told him to go get it. So Ted told him I was going with him to get it. We left to go get it. We smoke a blunt on the way back to Ted's house to get the car.

So we get the car and when we get in, Ted told me he had a song he wanted me to listen to by Fifty Cent. The name of the song was "How We Do" by Fifty Cent and the Game. So we are coming down the dirt road listening to the song. And when we get in the yard, Jason runs out of the house with no shoes on, and that was not like him. He told me to get in the back seat because someone had hit Lisa from behind. So I pull out my gun and cock it, and told him, "Let's go get them", because at the time I was thinking that somebody tried to rob her.

But it was a car wreck. She had five kids in the car. Three of them were hers and Jason's and two were Jordan's, Jason's brother. The person who hit them jumped out and ran. So Jason tells me to go find him and bring him back, and I would die trying because I looked up to him. So Jason, Jake (Jason's brother) and his girlfriend, Dave and I, we go looking for them. When we find them, it is Darrell and his brother, and they had called their aunt to come get them. They were getting in the car when we pulled up behind them. So Jason pulls Darrell out of the car and starts beating him and asks him why he hit them and ran. Darrell said he did not know what he was talking about.

Dave's got Darrell's brother with a .38 to his neck. So Jason told Darrell we were going to where the state trooper was at. So he put him in the back of the truck. I told him to lock the child safety lock so he could not jump out. But he did not do it, so Darrell tried to run. When he was running, I shot him in the leg with the same 40-caliber that Nolan had given me. I know I had hit him, so I go look for him, me and Jason. He was under a car in these Mexicans' yard. We tell him to come out. We were going to help him out and get him to the laws. So he gets from under the car and I start back to the truck, me and Jason. And when I look back, Darrell is going into the woods. I said that I was not going in there to get him.

So we go back to where Jason and his daddy and sister Liz and Lisa are at and we told Jason's daddy that I shot the boy. So he told me to go to Ted's until I hear something. So I got to Ted and ask if I can stay with him for the night and he told me yes. I told him I had shot Darrell. So the next morning, I told Ted I would see him at 710 Drag Strip. That was Sunday. When I get to Jason's, he tells me that Darrell died.

I told him I didn't do anything and he said, "That's right." So we are at the track chilling, drinking beer, and smoking weed. So now it is time to go home. And it is that Monday that I get locked up because of Jason. He had a tape recorder on me while we talked about what had happened. He asked me what I did with the gun, and I told him it was gone.

And that is why I am in prison. I am doing a

seventeen to twenty-one years bid because of a snitch. But I am going to stay strong and keep my head up and keep moving. I started walking the Red Road when I came to prison in September 2006. Before I started walking the Red Road, I was going down the Black Road at a speed I could not control. I hate that I had to come to prison to learn the way of life of my people. I wish that I would have been brought up in a long house or wigwam the way my people came up. I still got some things I got to learn to deal with: learning how to control the "wolf" that lives in me every day behind these walls. I almost got the chain on that wolf. When I am done, I will be at peace. I got to balance myself at all times.

My Brothers have worked with me very hard. It is time for me to step up and show them that their hard work has paid off. I love all my Brothers and hope I can share the knowledge that they have shared with me with the next generation. Wherever I will live in the "Iron House", I will share all the knowledge I can with them and teach them all I can about the Red Road. When I started walking the Sacred Hoop here at Alexander Correctional, I have never before felt the spirits like I have here. I enjoy being as one with my brothers and being with the Creator. Most of all, I know I'm well-loved when I am out smoking the sacred pipe with my Brothers, and with all the Native people who have died for us and carried on this way for 30,000 years so that we can live this way of life today. I wish I could have been there to fight with my people.

The only way I am at peace in here is when I am in the sacred hoop with the Creator and my Brothers of the Buffalo. I am working on being at peace at all times. It is hard for me to be behind the "Iron Gates", but I will make it with the Creator and my Brothers behind me no matter what. The more I read about my people and the more I think about some of the things that I have seen with the "Red Tail Hawk", I see that the Native way is the only way for me.

I thank the Creator first for allowing me to see this day. I thank everybody at Wake Forest University for helping us with this book. For their guidance, I thank all the two-legged, the four legged, the wing people, the water people, the four corners of the world, the plant people, and the rock people – all my relations.

I thank Thunder Wolf and Red Horse for their guidance and strength to push me to better myself and to help me fight that wolf. I appreciate that, Brothers.

I send out a "War Cry" to all my brothers and sisters in these "Iron Houses" to stay on the Red Road, to stay true to your walk of life. I send a prayer to all the families that are doing good and to those that are doing bad. You are in my prayers. That is how the Red Road has changed me. Maybe it was for a good reason that the Creator sent me to the "Iron House", to get on the Red Road, to find myself, to better myself, to help others also. I hope that my story will help other men to find their self and to better each other. I love you, my Brothers of the Buffalo.

Stay strong in your walk.

Aho.

Little Elk

Today, Tomorrow

Red Horse

Today, tomorrow no one knows, but death
will come, a time to ride the clouds of
the spirit world.

A time to fly in the places
where only the spirit can go.

Grandfathers, Grandmothers, watch over us,
until we also travel someday on the clouds
of the spirit world.

Circle of Life

Malcolm

My name is Malcolm. I was born on December 24th 1971. I was born in Laurinburg, Scotland County, NC. I lived in Hoke County all my life. I don't remember much until I was around five -- except that I was brought home in a Christmas stocking. When I was five years old, I remember my Mom saying that Dad was home from overseas in the military. It was Easter. After I saw him for a couple of hours, he was gone. My mother divorced him and married another guy. He was alright. He took me fishing and done things with me on occasion. I'll never forget, he had a little convertible midget car and I loved riding in it. While living with him for a couple of years, my Mom got pregnant with my brother. Come to find out it wasn't my stepdad. The father was actually my father. So I guess, this is to say that my mother had an affair with my real father while with my stepdad. I don't know how he took it, because we didn't know each other until some years later.

A couple of years go by, and Mom had a little girl, my sister, by my stepfather. During this time, my father is coming around trying to see us, my brother and me. I see him a couple of times. All that my mother tells me to do is that if I want something, to ask him for it. Even when he wasn't around, she would say every time I wanted something, "Call your father and ask him." So every time I saw him or he heard from me was when I wanted something. This wasn't all that often, because he drove a truck and was never in one place for very long.

When I was around nine or ten, my mother and stepfather separated and divorced. It was a major blow for me, because I had grown attached to him. I didn't want him gone. And then, to top it all off, my mother goes and moves another man in, my now to date Dad. I rebelled and showed out a lot. I even said that I wanted to live with my real Dad. That wasn't going to happen, because Mom ruled the roost. She supposedly kept us away from him, my brother and me, as punishment for him for not being with her and not paying her money for us (child support, I guess).

Sometime, while I was ten or eleven and while living with new stepdad, my real Dad comes around and asks to see my brother and me. Mom finally agrees for him to take us out to eat pizza the next day. I am so excited. Everything almost goes as planned. He takes us out to eat pizza alright, it's just that the pizza place happens to be in Oklahoma. This is where his mother and father live. Grandma and Grandpa are really excited to see us and that we'll be living with them. Dad told my brother and me that Mom said it was alright and that she'd be there soon, too. This is all I could ask for, living with my real Dad and my Mom coming, too. A kid's dream.

Well, my grandparents have a pond behind their house for us to fish, a boat that they say the next weekend we'll go out on in the big lake. They even enroll me in school. My first day at school, my brother doesn't want me to leave. He's still in diapers and doesn't know Dad or the grandparents. So Grandpa beats him with a belt, because he's crying because he doesn't want me to leave. That really threw me off of getting to know him too well. Who knew I'd come to regret this later?

A couple of weeks go by, and no Mom in sight until one day out of the blue, she pulls up in the yard and knocks on the door. Grandma doesn't let me see her and makes her leave. I don't understand what's going on. That afternoon, the police arrive and arrest my father for kidnapping. They allow my grandparents to keep my brother and me until a court proceeding straightens everything out. After a few weeks go by, we finally have to be in court. This whole time my real Dad has had to stay in jail until the day before court. The judge takes me and my brother into his chambers to talk to him and then to me. We didn't know what to say or what not to say.

Finally, the judge gives my mother custody and says we'll be living with her. I'll never forget seeing my Dad on the front steps of the Oklahoma Courthouse. I try to go and give him a hug and talk to him. He's crying and my mother will not allow me to go to him. He won't even speak to me while I'm trying to holler at him. I thought it was all my fault.

On the drive back to North Carolina, my mother explains a lot to me about things. I am still rather young, so I interpret them according to what I want to hear, mostly. She explains that my brother's last name, being different from mine, was the only reason that she got us back. She said Dad kidnapped him and that my brother wasn't my father's son, even though she knew he was. That's when I found out he was my whole brother and not just half-brother.

After we got back to North Carolina, we ended up moving around a lot. I started rebelling against all rules and basically everything. I set fire to a field at my grandparents' house on my mother's side. I didn't do anything in school. Got straight F's all the time, but passed all my grades up until the ninth grade. I'd forge my mother's name on papers from the school. I'd just do everything possible to make their adult life as miserable as I thought mine was. A new man was in the house trying to tell me what to do. He had two kids of his own that he got to see every other weekend and that he had to pay child support for. That left very little to survive on for our family. He held strong and saw it through, even though my mother was no walk in the park to live with, three kids and all.

And my brother could do no wrong what so ever. He'd get away with almost anything he did. If he and I did something wrong, I got in trouble. I was the oldest, I should know better. Oh well. Yeah, that caused a lot of friction between him, me, and my mother. She said he almost died shortly after he was born. Like that was supposed to explain it all and make it all right. Besides, I guess I should not have complained so much. My sister, even in diapers, caught worse havoc than I. Everything she did was wrong, and she would get punished in my stead. But I didn't look at it like that.

We didn't hurt for anything, we just didn't have anything extra. Always hand me downs, cheap everything. Forty pound box of chicken a week, but at least we got to eat. And they - the parents - took us on yearly vacations or weekend trips to the lake. But the whole time, for the longest time, I was waiting for this new stepdad to get put to the curb and for someone else to step in, so I never let him get too close. I really regret that now, because today he is a big part of my life. I just didn't know that then. This went on up until I turned fourteen years old.

I got a summer job, made money of my own, smoked weed for the first time. I didn't think I should have to go back to school. Mom caught me and my sister smoking cigarettes and made me eat one and swallow it, then smoke a whole cigar (inhaling it all), and beat the crap out of me. I know this doesn't sound all that bad, but it's hard to talk about all the punishments and beatings. They were sometimes really vigorous. One time, I was made to sit in an old car that was in the yard with all the windows up and with the temperature over one hundred degrees for over an hour. That hurt physically and emotionally.

Around the time of being thirteen and fourteen and fifteen, my aunt, who lived in Virginia, would allow me to come and spend a couple of weeks during the summer. She had a daughter six years older than I was and a son four years older. They didn't like me, because I was really rebellious and they really weren't (yet!). But I screwed that up, too. I stole a golf cart and rode it around the gated community they lived in and got caught. Mom drove over four hours to beat me that time. So back home I went. Finally, my Mom and stepdad bought some land and a trailer. No more moving around. But still I couldn't get off this road I was traveling.

Turning fifteen in the ninth grade really started my downfall. Up until now, I could have straightened up and really applied myself and possibly become someone.

Instead, I chose all the wrong people to hang around. Skipping school, and running away from home.

One day I remember, I skipped school. I rode the bus to school, then left campus. While away from school, my mother came to pick me up for a dentist appointment. Imagine her surprise and anger when I was away from school without her permission. That one still hurts!! Well, I failed the ninth grade, which was no surprise. If I wasn't skipping school, I was getting suspended, or paddled (something which they don't do anymore). Mom tried to change my schools and made me live with my uncle. I did the same things except that he grew pot in his well house, so being that I was in a higher grade in school and left before his twin sons, I would sneak in and take weed to school to smoke with my friends. Thankfully I never got busted for drugs at the time. So I quit school when I turned sixteen.

Mother said, "If you are not going to school, you're going to get a job or move out." I did both. I got a job and moved in with my cousin who moved down from Virginia. He liked me now that I could help pay his rent and buy our drugs. So I'm living with him and his wife for a little over a year, doing every drug known. Drinking was an everyday thing, too. As long as I could pay my way, buy drugs, and always babysit their three kids, I was a part of the family. We were always in need of money. I would go steal things so we'd have cash. I'd walk through the woods to my Mom's and take something to sell. For a while they didn't know it was me, but after a while it became obvious.

The first time I got arrested was because a friend and I were out so he could sell plasma. They wouldn't let me, so while walking around, I see a lady's purse just sitting in the front seat of a car. I took it and we went around to different country stores that trusted me to cash checks for me. I guess I had cashed six or seven hundred dollar worth of checks before the first one bounced. The stores that knew me gave me the chance to pay them back instead of pressing charges. I tried to begin with paying them back and then thought more of spending my money on myself. So they pressed charges. I got arrested in front of my cousins and their children. You would have thought I would have been embarrassed but, oh no, I thought I was cool.

I got lucky and got probation. For sentencing, I was facing thirty-five to forty years (forgery and theft). I went straight back to my cousins and got high. Being that I got slapped on the hand, I thought what the heck, why work all the time when I can just take what I want? Well, nothing too good lasts too long. After getting a ticket and losing my license for not paying the fine, my cousins and I moved. One weekend, we're going to Virginia to visit friends and family. Some friends come along with us, all the while doing drugs. While in Virginia at a friend's house, words get changed around and people get mad. A big fight starts and everyone heads back to North Carolina.

Upon returning, all trouble was of course blamed on me. Although ninety percent of things in my life are generally my fault, this particular time was not one of them. After the friends busted through the door to my cousin's place and beat me around a bit, I was informed that I had to leave. Best thing that could've happened. I moved back home with Mom, found a job, and end up hanging around this guy who gets me caught up in a quarrel with his girlfriend. I end up with a broken nose and a lot of aggravation.

During my healing, I met what turned out to be my first wife. She already had two kids, a boy, five years old, and a girl, four years old. I love both dearly to this day. The daughter, who was just beating histiocytosis (cancer of the bones) thought the world of me. The son, who was very ADD and had no male influences in his life, really bonded with me. I spent all my time with them. I started changing for the better.

So we move in together and everything seems like it is going to be just fine. Now without a permanent father figure in my life growing up, and their father not being a part of their life, we all had something in common. So to begin with, I tried to give them everything I didn't think I had. In '91, I found out I was going to have another daughter. I could not have been happier. Although I thought I had everything I wanted, so why not be able to do what I wanted also? So I started doing drugs again, behind everyone's back this time. Before, I didn't care who knew. Now I had an image to uphold. Well, to support a family and to do drugs took some kind of money. So I started doing criminal things again. I opened a bank account with fifty dollars and wrote seventy some thousand dollars in bad checks for stuff to resell for drugs and cash. Soon after my youngest daughter was born, I had a probation violation from my first charge ever.

In '92, at twenty years old, I get my first prison sentence. Three years under the old law, but all the same I'm scared. I do almost a year. I get in a lot of fights. One good thing is that I got my GED when I wasn't in the hole (segregation). I got out at the end of '95 and moved to Concord, NC to work. I ended up staying with some of my wife's distant family. My family stays where they are, waiting till I get things settled in. Well, the guy and his wife that I'm staying with are having family issues. While he works second shift, I end up sleeping with his wife. First time I've ever cheated on my wife. To this day my wife still doesn't know about this one.

I move back to where my wife and kids are staying, get a job, and on the surface everything seems like it's going to be fine. But under the surface, my surface that is, I'm going to pieces. I'm smoking pot all the time, going to bars after work, because now I'm of age and trying to see what I've missed being married and locked down at a young age. I've stopped spending all this quality time with my family, especially my kids.

I'm turning into everything I hated about my real father. My step son is really showing out with the ADD he had. He had to be hospitalized for a while. My marriage was in shambles, and my wife informs me she is pregnant again, my fourth child at the age of twenty two. It turns out to be a boy. I wouldn't have changed anything to have my boy.

Well, things only got worse. I had no one to blame but myself. I chose the path I was walking. I started smoking crack now. Spending every dime I made and whatever I could steal to get by. So my wife finally has enough. I keep the kids at home one weekend and she goes to visit her sister-in-law out of town. Her husband went to prison in Louisiana, and she's with another man. While visiting with them, my wife hooks up with her oldest son's Dad. Although I had cheated already, my wife didn't know. She just thought I had flirted with numerous other girls at topless bars. I was irate. So we move again.

We try to work through our differences, because we love each other and have children together. I get a different job, but end up having to stay out of town in Jacksonville, NC, at the military base. I'm in a motel that has a bar. I'm drinking and doing drugs with one of the friends working with me. While one friend is asleep, the other friend and I take his keys and go get hookers and crack.

I get stopped by the law and are taken to jail for having no license. Then I had to explain why I took my friend's car. So during this time, my wife and I find out that her stepfather is molesting our oldest daughter. He gets ten years on probation. Shortly after that, my wife and I separate for a few weeks. One weekend, I have the kids and have my Mom babysit while I go to a bar. My wife is there with her ex. I have way too much to drink and I leave. I go outside and end up in a fight with the bouncer. The cops get called. Long story short, I end up with a DUI and get found guilty.

All throughout '91-'95, I'm getting in all kinds of trouble: everything from breaking and entering to driving charges, to possession of stolen goods, and especially bad checks. I opened another bank account and wrote over forty thousand dollar worth of bad checks. Now my credit's ruined. I have a criminal record with multiple felonies. Next, I started a business with my best friend in '95. We had it going good. A lot of work and money was pouring in. But I had all these past crimes and new charges coming from everywhere it seemed. So for two years, I was leading a double life: one of a working husband and father and the other a business owner/drug addict. Everything seemed to be going fine.

After handling all my new charges and not getting prison time, I go to see my probation office after two years of not contacting him. He puts me in custody. But, being the pothead that I was, I keep a half ounce of pot in my crotch, so if he did lock me up, the cell block could get high. It just so happened that the jail had changed its search procedure since I'd last been arrested. They found it and gave me a box car sentence to the one I was getting for the violation. So from February 14th '99 to December 1st of 2000, I was in prison again. While doing this time, I had a chance to think about what I was doing to my wife and kids. What really made me see myself was when I had work release and home passes and got busted back in for a dirty urine test.

I left with an honor grade work release and went to medium custody, Johnston County, where I met an Indian guy who prayed with a pipe and asked me one day if I'd like to join him in a circle. I always knew I was part Indian, just never knew or understood what that meant to me. For almost a year, he taught me things and explained so much. For that short length of time, I was at peace within myself. I switched camps and went straight back to the way I was except that I contacted my wife and told her I wouldn't be coming home to her. I was tired of hurting her and didn't think I'd ever change. The absolute biggest mistake I have ever made and will ever have made.

I ended up getting out of prison and being the father that my real father was: never there for my children. I moved to Virginia where I met my second wife. One who didn't mind who and what I was. She was the spitting image of me, except a woman. She had three daughters, and although I never stopped thinking about or loving my children, I was there for someone else's children, just not mine anymore. I ended up strung out on crack again and stole someone's checks. I got ten years in prison. I only had to do two. Got out, got strung out again, violated probation, and caught a new charge. Done two more years in Virginia and then came back to North Carolina to do a habitual felon sentence.

During my incarcerations and learning outside these walls, I learnt about my heritage off and on. For the last eleven to twelve years, I have practiced my Native American Religion and can honestly say that it is due to this that I have changed, and never to go back to what I once was. I have lost so much that I can never get back. My oldest daughter has four kids now. My oldest son is in prison for sixty some years. I believe that if I would have been there for him, he wouldn't be in prison now. My blood daughter just graduated from high school. My son is sixteen. None of them will talk to me because of the disappointment. Maybe when I will get out, they'll see that I've changed and I can again be a part of their life. Walking the circle of life has shown me that I cannot change what was. What I make out of life with the Great Creator and the Circle of Life has two roads: one red, which is good, one black, which is not all good. Where they meet in the middle is balance. Losing everything I had made me realize a few things. Like what is was like for my ancestors to have everything taken away from them and how I lost it all because of stupidity and drugs. Dying is not something I fear anymore, but what people remember about me means a lot. I just hope after all I've done that I have time left to do things in the eyes of my people and ancestors that will overlay most of the rest. Walking the Red Road with the help of my brothers and sisters of all creation I've seen this, maybe someone else will, too. Just because you think you have it bad, someone has it worse. By helping others, I've helped myself.

This is my life story, almost complete, and all very true.
Aho. Mitakuye Oyasin.
Hoka Hey,
Malcolm

UNDERSTAND

Red Horse

Understanding is the pain of knowledge
Knowledge is the pain of understanding.
But do we truly understand?
Do we understand why a person picks up a gun to kill?
Why people try to kill themselves?
Why we let drugs rob us and
Let other things steal the light of our soul?
Do we truly understand the passing of days and nights?

To gain knowledge and to understand,
we must allow the Creator's spirit to lead us by his loving hands.
Then we'll gain the knowledge to understand.

MY LIFE

Jesus A. Campos

My journey has not stopped yet. I feel myself searching for the purpose of my being. The images of those before me keep on popping inside my mind. Their messages are not clear to my clouded mental state. It's as if the mystical forest inside my mind hasn't been explored thoroughly. Through the bark of these magnificent trees runs a spirit that lacks connection. These remarkable creations hold a power that we fail to embrace.

My lack of ancestral knowledge can be blamed on so many things but at the end of the day, it's my fault. Once I accepted the truth, and blamed myself for not listening to my elders, I decided to teach myself and asked the Creator for guidance and for Him to allow me to understand my roots. Understanding my past is the only way I can understand my future. What today's society taught me came from books that were created to cover only what the conquistadores taught to be right.

My name is Jesus. I am the oldest son of Armando A. C. and Alicia R., my dear mother and father whom I love very much. My father passed away when I was a very small child and my mother did the best she could to raise me. She did her best, which I appreciated deeply as a young loving child, but in her mind it still wasn't enough.

As my body developed and I got older, so did my five finger habit or the "Snatch and Run" technique. Of course, as an innocent child I only did what I could do to help my poor mother. Sometimes, I would come home to her with a glittering gold watch. I would tell her that "I found it." I would shrug my tender shoulders and smile slightly. I guess she knew what was up, but she would block it out of her mind due to the fact that she loved me and I could do nothing wrong in her eyes. Picking up scrap metal and beer cans was another one of my little hustles that helped put pesos in my pocket and food in my belly. Every now and then, we would hustle the guichos - rich people- of their change by putting up a show juggling balls and beer bottles that had been painted with spray cans with our hands.

Chispa, René and Nancy, Chispa's sister, on whom I had a bad crush since the first time I met her, were the first ones to show me love as soon as I sat foot in Diablo's Territory. I remember that they were playing soccer on the gravel road when I arrived. They invited me to play. I accepted with no hesitation, eager to make new friends. Monterrey was a very beautiful city, and admiring its beauty from the top of the mountain was breathtaking. As the night hit, Nancy, Chispa, René, and I laid on our backs, staring at the sky and wondering what it would be like to fly to the moon and what we would do if we ever got a chance to do it. The crickets chirped and the chicharras made their unmistakable sound as our minds unfolded into a world of our own. The connection was felt as we shared the same dream. It was one of those feelings I would not change for anything. Innocent, yet awake to our surroundings, we closed our eyes for a moment and felt the night breeze on our eyelids until Chispa said, "Your Mom is calling you, chuy."

The Cuevas was a place we wouldn't dare to go, because it was in enemy territory. However, one day we felt crazy and decided to go. I don't remember the exact history behind the Cuevas. What I do remember is that they belonged to the other hood. But as we made our way up toward Las Cuevas, we came in contact with a Desfile de Danzas dedicated to La Virgen Maria de Guadalupe.

I was happy to see them, because memories of my native Coahuila paced through my mind and made me realize that my culture was still there in Monterrey. It is a city way different from my small Ranchito de la Rosita, where I grew up around people who held the same rituals and Dansas to honor our ancestors. I guess back then I was just happy to see some fun around our rough neighborhood. My heart beat side by side with the drums and my feet stomped at the same rhythm as the feathers adorning the dancers' heads that bounced up and down. The clacking sounds of the wooden bows and the shells that tapped against shiny golden cascabeles sent a feeling of freedom through my physical self that made me feel elevated. My rubber chanclas, dusty from the dirt, gave my dancing feet support as I danced to the sound of drums and maracas. My eyes wide open and fixed on the paintings on the dancers' faces, trying to lock eyes and make a connection with every single one of them. Finally, one of the females looked and winked at me, with her two long braids bouncing off her shoulders. I stopped dancing and my face turned red. But she smiled and she kept on going. I looked to my side to look for my friends, but they were gone. Later I found out that they had bounced to Las Cuebas without me.

The party was jamming and the Diablos were everywhere. Bright red shirts and black jeans, adjusted against their bodies, singled them out from the crowd. La Tropa Vallenata boomed out of the speakers and people enjoyed themselves as they moved their feet rhythmically to the sound. "Andale, let's dance," Nancy pleaded as she tugged at my hand gently, but with a little force. I wasn't a great dancer when it came to La Tropa Vallenata, but I could do a little something. Truth is, I wasn't comfortable because it was always us four, with nobody else around, just us dancing. "Nell altrado" I said to her with the best smile I could manage but, at the end, she convinced me. I'm sure you vatos can relate. I held her close because, from what I learned from watching my prima Erica dance, the trick was not to step on your partner's toes and to hold her as tight as you could and to dance on the same spot. My cheek was pressed against hers and my palms moist from her heat, flat against hers. I was in another world on the moon and now that I had set foot on it, what was I to do? Even though I had thought about it before, I never really came up with an answer. So, I just danced on it and enjoyed the experience to the fullest. My young mind was way out in space and my heart in her pocket. I rubbed my cheek slowly to one side against hers and pecked the beauty mark on top of her upper lip. She shied away and then surprised me with the sweetest kiss that my lips will remember forever.

When I walked through the door of our humble home, my Mom was standing on one side and my stepdad was seating on the bed with a belt in his hands. I looked at my Mom looking for help, but she just shook her head and looked at the ground. My stepdad asked me where I had been, grabbed me, spun me around, and whipped me with his belt. My tears flowed out of my eyes and screams left my mouth. Not because of the whipping, but because I didn't receive any help from my mother. The only protector I trusted and loved had denied her help as this stranger laid hands on me.

I held the leaf against my nose enjoying the sweet mint aroma it produced. My friends were at school and wouldn't come back till later. It was my daily routine to just climb the mountain in search of things to entertain myself with. I placed the leaf inside my mouth and sucked the minty juice of it because to me, it tasted good. I looked around in search of something to do. I found nothing. I walked over yellow, orange, and dried up brown leafs. I made my way towards the tree whose leaves I'd been stepping on and sat against its gray trunk. Looking at the city below, I started to imagine a different life. I picked one of the dried twigs and started to tap my knee with it as I hummed a Dansa song. A small bird landed on a branch right on top of me. I stopped humming and looked up at its abdomen and beak. His song was sweet at first but then - for some reason - it irritated me, so I threw the twig I held in my hand at it hoping to hit him, but I missed. And he kept on singing as if nothing mattered. I just smiled and searched for another twig to throw at him.

"Nobody's going to see us" I told Nancy. "Why you so scared?" "Because she's a girl," Chispa said laughing. "Ouch". He rubbed his arm on the same spot Nancy had just pinched him. I held the Faro in between my lips as I stroke the match against the box and watched it ignite into a small blue flame. I placed the flame at the Faro's tip and puffed. My small lungs couldn't handle the toxic smoke and they forced me to cough it out. "I thought you knew how to do it," Nancy said with a skeptical look on her face. "I…do…I…," I coughed like crazy. That's what I did, and the truth is that I had never done it, but I'd seen my grandpa and stepdad do it and it looked easy. "Your…turn…," I said in between coughs passing the Faro to Chispa who was cracking up with hands on his belly and all. He stopped and looked at me with a devilish look. I looked at Nancy and waited for the moment to get my breath back.

"Muchachos!" One of our lady neighbors stood over the blue barrels that sheltered us. We looked up and then took all off at the same time like race horses as soon as the gates pop open. My heart was beating fast and the blood in my veins raced toward it, giving it more fuel. The rocks under my feet gave me the traction I needed to reach my destination- the wilderness. My heart was pounding hard as if it were trying to break through my ribs and out of my chest. "Diosito, please don't let mi mama find out" I prayed silently with my hands placed against each other against my mouth and nose, as I imitated the posture of the Virgin Mary.

I said my prayers and waited a while for a sign. Nothing came. But still I knew that God was out there somewhere, and busy. So, I figured that I had to confront this little problem by myself. I pushed myself off the ground with both hands, and looked around. My heart was beating normally now and my face was back to its normal brown color from the scared fiery red that had invaded it earlier. I climbed a tree for a little fun and sat on one of the branches that looked like it could hold my weight. I looked up at the sky and a picture of my grandmother appeared in the clouds. Her smile was warm and her beautiful curly hair surrounded her face making her appear like the angel she was. I missed her hugs and kisses and just everything about her. My lips quivered and my tears yearned to escape from under my eye lids, but I refused to let them escape.

When I arrived home, that same night, my aunt Ceci was there in front of my Mom delivering the news about me smoking. I looked at my Mom and waited. Her jet black hair was shining in the light that came from the gas lamp sitting on the table. She looked at me with a mad expression but, to my surprise, she didn't hit me.

If I had a relationship with God as a child, I couldn't tell you that I really knew who He was. All I know is that my grandmothers would always scream "Jesus" or "Dios mio!" whenever something went wrong and so I picked it up. Mi mama Cruz - my Mom's mother - was a Protestant ChristIan and I would see her go to the Cultos all the time, but I never went with her. Mi abuelita Tita - my father's Mom- however, she was a very strict Catholic woman. Rosarios hung from almost every place inside her house. Pictures of a pale Jesus and La Morenita Virgen Maria were on every wall. One thing that I recall asking someone was "why is La Virgencita darker than Jesus if that's her Son?" My grandmother would've flipped on me if I had asked her this innocent question, but this person simply answered, "Because he looks more like his father." That answer right there has stuck with me forever, because I had no memories of my father inside my mind to go back to. My mother never talked about him, and I didn't know what he looked like. But I was happy to know that I had taken on his features and that maybe, like Jesus, I looked like my father. I would imagine how he looked and wondered if he still remembered me wherever he was.

My abuelita Tita sat me on her lap and wrapped me inside her reboso on a warm morning and sung songs softly for me to enjoy. She rocked the mecedora back and forth with her feet and rubbed my arm tenderly. Her songs always gave me hope, and to my life they gave more than meaning. They gave love and more than a child, living in poverty, would ask for. She stopped rocking and my eyes popped open against her chest. She pulled an atalaya and started to read slowly about the teachings of Jesus and how his purpose was to help all humanity. I could care less. All I wanted to do was listen to her voice and fall asleep in her arms, which I did eventually.

For many reasons, mi abuelita Tita felt that living with my mother was not good for me and I, myself, though a young child, felt like my Mom didn't need me to provide and help her anymore, because she had another man in her life. My grandmother and I boarded a train back to my beloved Rosita Coahuila, the place I had dreamed of going back to plenty of cold nights. I had missed the estanques, pilas, tajos, and its deserts. The fields of corn which were my favorite playground and of course my other family members.

It was then that I was able to get back to school. I loved school and the fact that my old friends were still there to receive me with open arms. My friends Cerrucho and lran, and my cousin Nahun were the ones I always hung around with. My tia Paty had two kids with my tio Piporro, Anita and Tonito. La Morena- that's what we called Anita due to her dark skin and dark eyes- and El Trompudo- that's what we called Tonito due to his big lips- lived with my Grandma and Grandpa and their parents in the house that holds many childhood memories. Valeria also lived there with us. She was the daughter of mi tia Nena who was living in the U.S.

When we arrived, mi tia Paty was there with her escuincles waiting for us as we unboarded the train. They helped us with our luggage and we walked under the pinabetes and crossed the small bridge, covered in red chipping paint, toward my grandmother's house. I was moved by the warm welcome and my eyes got watery.
The next day, I walked toward mi tio Borrao's house to visit. Mi tio Borrao is someone I love and admire, still to this day, simply because he is a hard working family man. He was ensillando his horse to la carrucha, getting ready to go work on his land. "A Ji Jo…Como estas mi

chuy", he exclaimed surprised and with joy in his voice. I couldn't say anything. I just ran and wrapped my hands around his waist and pressed my right cheek against his belly. He picked me up, placed me on top of the carrucha and we were gone toward la labor. The bumpy ride was my delight. To me it felt like riding a roller coaster. I admired the houses we passed by, some white, some pink, others blue, with most of them decorated with macetas hanging from strings. Others were decorated with little colorful birds, singing for freedom, inside their cages. Suddenly my eyes stopped on the house that my mother and I had lived in before moving to Monterrey. My father had left that house for my mother and me when he passed away. It was the only memory I had of my father and that was the only reason I loved that house, even though it was a small house, made out of adobe. It leaked so badly when it rained that it felt like it had no roof at all. I loved that house more than anything, because my father had built it for me. My mother had sold that house, not knowing that my soul and spirit had gone with it.

Mi tio Borrao parked right beside the parcela and got ready to work. He handed me a brown sack with what looked like little blue pebbles. He told me it was fertilizer. He placed his hands on my shoulders and said "Esta tierra ha sido trabajada por nuestra gente desde hace mucho tiempo" ("This earth has been worked by our people for a long time"). He turned to face the rows of tilled dirt and said, "Ahora pon attencion mijo porque un dia tu tambien lo haras." ("Now pay attention … because one day, you will do it").

Mi abuelita Tita held her rosario tightly as she prayed, kneeling in front of a portrait of La Virgen. Candles burned slowly as their light shone against the teary faces of the devotees. I looked around searching for the tamales that would be served after all the praying was over. I could already smell their sweet odor mixed with that of atole. My knees were aching and I was bored to death. My Grandma's strength was something to admire -

you had to. She was an ill woman, strong in heart but weak physically, but somehow her faith made her forget her illnesses. When she knelt in front of her Protectora, she felt rejuvenated and strong.

It was moments like these that kept me from complaining about going to church at times. That's how I know I got the spirit I carry inside of me: it is from her, because she was a fighter. Even now I know she's near me after travelling the Milky Way into the next life. I know she still kisses my forehead before I go to sleep. I didn't know it then, but it would be days like these that would lead me to search for spiritual stability in the future.

"Nieve?" I asked in disbelief as we ran home to get our jackets. "Si. Nieve!" He said laughing as little snowflakes crashed against his face making it turn red, especially his nose and cheeks. I opened the door to my Grandma's house and searched for my jacket. I'd never seen snow fall from the sky and to keep it real, I didn't want to go back outside because I was scared to get buried alive under this so-called nieve. A knock on the door called me and I ran toward the door. Iran came into view as soon as I opened the door. "Vamanos!" He yelled and took off towards the planta where a big rosario was being held, because to the people, La Virgen was baptizing them from the heavens. It was a miracle - the fact it was snowing - and it could only had come from La Virgen.

We arrived just in time to drink atole and eat tamales, buñuelos and all the good stuff. The food was the only blessing we cared about at the time, but somehow, I knew it meant something bigger. The air was cold due to the low temperature, but the heat and the togetherness created by being all huddled inside one of the bodegas in La Planta was something we couldn't ignore. The smiles and warm conversations were a part of community growth and friendship. Like ants, we worked hard for the well-being of the young and elderly.

I can recall many incidents where I'd been

disciplined by someone other than my Mom and family members. This was what was being placed inside my heart and I, for some reason, wouldn't appreciate it. The stubbornness of the city and bad habits I'd picked up in Monterrey had followed me to Coahuila.

I held the truck my Mom had given me at one point for the Dia de Reyes as if it held the answers to my life. It was a big red truck with four barrels on its back. I believe it was an oil truck. I hadn't unwrapped it yet. Days, weeks, maybe months had passed and it was still wrapped in clear plastic. I was so scared to break it as to even make a little scratch on it. My mother had given it to me and to me, it was a reassurance. I ran my fingers over the plastic, asking it questions like "Is this right?" "Will my Mom be ok?" "Will my grandmother also be ok?" "What about my little sisters?" The truck didn't move or speak. It just sat in my lap and stood still. I was looking for answers. My grandmother had just told me that I had to leave with my uncle Beto to the U.S. Even though I was young, I still had to make decisions that would affect the lives of many people. I decided that it was best for me to go with him and make a future for myself. I wrote a letter for my Mom describing how I felt and other things I can't recall. All I know is that a piece of my heart lay in every line I wrote down. Next thing I know, I was on the back of my Grandpa's truck on my way toward the border.

Once across the border, the real task came: shaking off the border patrol and minute men who patrolled the area carefully, looking for people like us. My tia Paty, my uncle Beto's wife, whom I learned to love like a second mother, is a very strong woman. She had that old way kind of thinking and walked with dignity. She was searching for them also as she held on to my uncle's hand tightly. I held on with an iron grip as my tender hand was being squeezed by my uncle Beto's strong fingers. There was another man with us, but I don't remember his face or his name.

We walked inside the motel and sat down. I

rushed towards the restroom to wash my hands and face. I stepped inside and turned the lights on. When I reached over the sink to turn the water on, I noticed some chocolates sitting on the sink. I snatched them up and place them inside my jeans pocket. I was so happy I rushed back out and sat on the bed. I was dazing off and I cuddled on the bed ignoring my aunt's screams. She was complaining about not being able to find any soap. On that note I fell asleep.

Riding through the hot Arizona desert, the temperature was hot enough to melt your scalp off your head. I was fanning my face with both of my hands and wiping sweat off with my shirt's collar. I was bored and really hot. I pressed my head against the windshield and stared at whatever my eyes would set themselves upon. My sweaty forehead bumped slightly against the glass from the trembling of the car caused by the traction. Then I remembered that I had some chocolates in my pocket so I figured I eat one. I took one of my pocket and offered one to my aunt, trying to be polite. She looked at me and said "Those aren't chocolates! Those are soaps!" They burst out laughing and I just looked at the soap embarrassed.

"God has a purpose for all of us", my grandmother used to tell me. I was never sure what God was or who he was and what made people love him. All I knew was that Jesus looked like him and that La Virgencita was his mother. I never knew how Catholicism began in Mexico or who introduced it to my people. All I knew was that El Padre had to be respected, because he represented the church and that's what my elders said. No arguing was allowed, so I never asked questions. The only proof I had about the Aztecs being our people was what my homies had tattooed on their arms, backs, legs, chest and the Low Rider Art Magazines I used to look at. But they couldn't tell me anything more. My curiosity grew and I knew I had to learn about my ancestors. Somehow… some way.

The truth cannot be told to those who won't

accept it. In the end, it will be a waste of your time. If you seek truth, you will find truth. This can be achieved by using your right and left hemispheres of the brain. Because then you will be walking with a balanced, open mind. People sometimes say things happen due to coincidence, but what about purpose, the purpose of one's life? What are the most valuable functions of that purpose? When our body is of one accord with our minds, the respect for our own capabilities grows. The mystical planes that are waiting for us to board them are waiting. These planes will show us and lead us to a new beginning.

"Come on, just give it a try… it will be fun, you'll love it." The elderly woman spoke to me with such a happiness I had never seen before, but at the same time, I found this very annoying. Sleepy and tired, from a night of heavy partying and drinking, I wasn't trying to hear that message. "Alright. I'll go," I said staring at her trough the crack on the door. Even though it was a lie, I was trying to be respectful and I was hoping she would leave as soon as I said this. "Ok. Then here," she handed me a pamphlet and smiled. "Just remember that Jesus loves you." I grabbed the pamphlet out of her hand, took notice of her smile and closed the door. I walked back inside my room, then threw the pamphlet inside the trashcan. I lay down beside some girl and went back to sleep.

She was standing against the wall behind the bulletproof glass. My uncle Beto pointed her out to me. She was crying, biting her knuckles, and shaking uncontrollably. Her beautiful eyes were stained with pain and her tears left a trail that could not be erased with time. I couldn't believe that she had come to visit me in jail. I mean that's what you expect when society makes you look like the lowest of the lowest. Her name is Kay, the woman I had come to love for many years but couldn't be with due to some bad circumstances. She came and sat down after my uncle left. Her tears were flowing harder and harder, dropping into my heart, making a hollow spot inside it. “Hey,” she said weakly, staring at me through salty tears. “Don’t cry, baby” I spoke into the phone “That’s the last thing I want you to do for me.” She wiped her tears off and smiled because she knew that I was being sincere. We talked for a while and her words were comforting to me. She told me that she loved me. I believed her, even though in my heart there was pain and hurt. I believed things would be alright, because as my Grandma said, “Love overcomes everything.” I rushed back to my cell and began to see everything from a different perspective. First, hope inside my heart began to grow due to my acceptance of the love people around me offered. The negation of this love at first was killing my dreams and aspirations. The acceptance of this love made me realize that the people who loved me expected the same back and, until then, I had been selfish. I read the Bible to find comfort in my cell. All this that started inside my heart was a thing called curiosity. Who wrote this book? Where does the name Bible come from and who is Jesus for real?

The love people expressed to have for Jesus was a mystery to me. How can you love someone you don’t know and how can you accept African teachings taught by Europeans? Egypt, Ethiopia-Cush, and all these other places mentioned in the Bible are nowhere near Mexico. None of them. So this made me skeptical about a lot of things in the Bible. Didn’t my people have books of their own? Later I found out that only four are still in existence. They are called codexes. The rest were burnt by the Spanish conquistadores. I found out about many things that were kept from me so that I would just go along with the norm. Of course I believe in God, the one Divine Creator. What I don’t agree with is the term religion.

When I talked to my aunt Paty on the phone, I told her I’d been studying the Bible. “So you’re going to come out of there with one under each armpit.” She laughed. It was a joke - I knew that - but I figured she would talk to me a little about it and show me a little more than what I knew. She instead changed the subject and we went on to another topic. Being in jail really didn't give me much to talk about and the options we had were basic everyday things. None matter though, because they have nothing to do with the outside world.

I took my time and studied the Bible. Being locked down for hours inside my cell, I didn't have anything better to do. The Bible was my escape. It took me to places I had never pictured in my life. Cities composed of gold, kings with treasures no other men had ever seen, and Zion where God's throne is located. Picturing these places and the rewards I would get just for believing in God's son made me believe even more.

I was sitting in jail facing life for a first degree murder and attempted murder. Only seventeen years old, and looking for the right guidance because the life I'd been living wasn't good at all. I had stayed in a state of isolation throughout my entire life. I felt like I couldn't trust anybody. Youth and stubborn drugs were my only counselors. The bad images inside my head had guided me into a cage of ignorance. Life as I knew it before drugs hit my system was gone. The images of that night crept back slowly into my head day and night as I tried to forget. The fact that I had taken someone's life was too much for my immature brain. Inside the jail, with no drugs to block out the hurt, my mind started to function in a wholly different manner. The realization of my actions was eating me slowly and it made me weak.

"God made me deaf" I said to my brother Rosas, a ChristIan brother who had been mentoring me and keeping me out of trouble. He helped me to stand firm and not let ignorant fools get to me. "I'm dead serious, homie. I just prayed to him and asked him to make me deaf to all the noise out here in the dayroom and he did." Though I didn't see myself as a ChristIan, this experience had changed my perspective on things. God existed and he didn't play games -- for real. "Ya ves" ("Now you see"), Rosas said calmly. "I told you."

The day of my trial came fast and all my family members were there. Seeing their sad faces was enough to make my heart fall to the pit of my stomach. When I looked to my right, my heart died as I watched the victim's mother crying uncontrollably. Her eyes fixed straight ahead of her, letting the tears flow freely. I couldn't take it, because I knew I'd caused it and I couldn't bring her son back. Even though I wished I could… I couldn't. The face of my mother appeared before me and I could see her going through the same pain. Her son was going to jail facing a life without parole sentence, and she was too far away to hold him and give him comfort. I hadn't seen my Mom for ten years and I rarely spoke to her, but when I did, I would cry afterwards. Sometimes I wouldn't even want to talk to her, because the pain was too much to bear. She would always ask me, "When are you coming back?" and all I could say was, "Soon." And the tears of this woman were tearing me apart, because now I understood the pain I'd caused.

I was sentenced to life in prison with no chance of parole. The tears exploded from my family's eyes and the screams shattered my soul to pieces, but I knew I couldn't change God's will, so I just accepted it. With tears running down my cheeks, I was escorted out the court room. I thanked the Sergeant for his assistance and his supportive words and was gone.

My spirit was shattered, but one thing I do thank God for doing was getting me close to my family. The first time my aunt and my uncle came to see me – the ones who raised me - I tried to shake my uncle's hand, but he slapped it away and gave me a big bear hug. And this man whom I had always looked up to because of his strength was crying on my shoulders. It took me by surprise to see him like that and it was then that I understood how much he loved me. My aunt hugged me as well and I saw the same thing inside her eyes. My stubbornness has made me blind to the love they had offered me before, but in my heart I was always thankful. I never found a way to say it, because I had never learned how to, but I'm sure they felt it whenever I tried.

Back in prison, I saw one of the Rastas wearing a tam with the red, gold and green on it. A dream I've had rushed back inside my head. I was alone walking through the most amazing place I've had ever seen, with trees and flowers of all types. I was alone hurling through obstacles like I was training for an army of some sort. I landed safely after handling the last hurdle. I looked around and found myself in the middle of beautiful palm trees, vegetation of all sorts, and the water was of the clearest blue specimen. Birds sang and flew about all around. Then a deep hole swallowed me and I fell into the deep. There was a pole in the middle and I held on for dear life. I asked Jah to help me and he didn't answer for the first three times. Then, I heard his voice. Powerful like thunder and sharp was his word. What we discussed is between me and Him, but after that, I was on that beautiful place again. Then a rainbow appeared and its colors were a radiant red, gold, and green. I believe in dreams. Many of my friends can testify that they come true. Sooner or later, they become reality. So I know Jah gave me this gift of dreams and so far they have all come true. I followed my dreams and stepped to my Rasta Brothers and ever since then, I've dedicated my life to teaching others about my roots and the roots of my ancestors.

There are many drums, but one heartbeat. The drums represent all Native people. Even in the Bible it says that there are many mansions. I consider myself a brother of all races because in the end, we all belong to one race... the human race. I thank my Rasta brothers for teaching me about the Aztecs, Mayas, and the Hopi. Now I will learn the ways of my ancestors and follow their Native teachings.

My life has opened a new chapter. The Creator has called me to walk the Red Road.

WISDOM INSIDE A CAGED SOUL

Jesus A. Campos

A large cage engulfs my eyes, formed by metal diamonds,
Erasing the visions I hold as I gaze across it.
Purity at one time filled my inner self.
Ghostly fog now enters my pupils, blinding my purpose.

Hope is not lost until our life is gone.

Beads of sweat make a stop on my brows and wait for my hand.
Scrolls of life exist in every face's wrinkle,
Notes of wisdom jingle in every gray hair.

The sun kisses my skin to remind me of who I am,
The sky watches me with deep blue eyes.
A soft whistle from a bird's beak soothes my mind
Another is placed to disperse through the sky.

I once heard screams that were cries, and
Some that were pride.

They navigated through the city trying to hide,
Ashamed at the way people look at each other.
Colors blind their eyes from their true brothers.

A breast that cradles the face of a child
nurtures a life inside with not yet awakened mind.

For now I sleep,
but will I awake inside another ghetto?

MY LIFE STORY

Strong Bow

I was born on August 16, 1987. I'm twenty-two years old now. At the time of my birth, my mother and father were raising me, my two brothers, and my sister. My sister is the oldest, she's thirty now. She used to keep us while both our parents went to work. But before they left the house, they would tell us, "Don't make a lot of noise." Little did we know that they had the next door neighbor listening, and when both our parents got off from work, we got our tail a spanking because we messed up the whole house. We had toys and paper everywhere. Not too long after that, we moved to a big trailer park named Quail Run in Clinton, NC, my hometown. It took time for me to get used to a new environment. At the time, I was in first grade, being a good little boy. I had anything I asked for if it wasn't too expensive.

In 1995, my parents split up, so my Daddy would come around every blue moon. He never sat down with me and had a father and son conversation. My mother didn't either, so I was running back and forth, with different people keeping me. That went on until I wanted to stay with my Grandma. Everybody used to say she's Indian, because she was real light, but I didn't know. She made sure that I had a full stomach, clothes to wear to school, and my aunt made sure that I would do my homework each and every day.

That was until my Daddy moved in with them. He was on drugs really bad. He started stealing from us, eating all of our food up to the point that we had to hide it from him. Then he used to tell me that I don't have to go to school if don't want to go. So I used to be at home all the time watching TV instead of going to school. I used to think that it was cool not going to school and hanging out at home, but when I finally went to school again, I had to go get tutoring. So I failed third grade not once, but twice, because not going to school happened again. Not too long after that, I went and spent the week with my mother. She was crying, because she heard that Social Services were going to send me to a foster home if I continued to miss school.

So when I went back, I was doing an assignment and got called to the office. When I went in there, it was the Assistance Principal and some white lady I hadn't seen before. They told me that I wouldn't be in trouble. Then the sheriff came and followed us to my mother's house. When my sister came out, she told them that my mother was gone and wanted to know what was going on. My window on the passenger side was rolled down, so my sister wanted to come and talk to me, but the lady rolled the window up and backed up out of our yard. I was crying, because I thought I wasn't going to see my family ever again. I cried for hours and hours. They tried to give me candy and different food to eat. I didn't feel like eating anything.

I waited in the Social Services office for three and a half hours until they took me to the foster home. I wanted my mother, that's all I used to say. I moved in with this old lady and her two grandchildren. I felt abandoned and thought nobody cared about me. My mother wasn't fighting to get me back, but a month later, I got off the school bus and saw the case worker car in the yard. When I came in, they told me to pack my clothes. I asked, "Where I'm going?" The case worker told me that wherever I will go, I'm going to like it the whole ride. I kept asking until she pulled in my aunt's yard. I was so happy I hugged her and my cousin so tight. It felt like I had been gone forever.

I got enrolled back in school, doing my homework every day. If I made good grades, I got a new video game and new shoes, basically anything I wanted. My aunt is a Christian, so I was in church every Sunday. I never did pay attention to what the preacher was talking about, because I'll fall asleep, but I was young. I didn't know any better. My aunt used to blow me out for that.

Then I got to where if I see grown-ups talking, I'll like to cut in. I got broke from doing that. One day, we got a call from my mother. She wanted to come and see me. I wanted to say no, because I had so much anger built up against her and my father. Still, I was happy to see her. I just couldn't accept the fact that she chose drugs over her children.

A couple of years later, in 2001, my grandmother got sick and was sent to the Chapel Hill hospital. My aunt went and visited her. When they got back, they said she was doing really well. So the next day, I was going to see her. About eleven o'clock the night before the visit, we got a phone call from the hospital, saying she was not going to make it. My brother and I were the first one to get there. She was in ICU on a breathing monitor. When the rest of the family got there, we all came to the conclusion to pull the plug so that she would suffer no more.

It hit me all at once. I started smoking weed, drinking, not caring about anything. It's like I lost a part of myself. She was my mother, my father. And I went and moved in with my mother again. Enrolled back in school and running the streets. Never did my homework until I got to school the next morning. Thinking it was cool. Then I started hanging out with my two cousins. All we used to do is drink and smoke every day until one day, they stole a truck, came to my house and picked me up. We were joy riding, speeding, stealing pool tables and guns. It became an addiction because we had not got caught for it at the time. We thought that if we did this, we could do just about anything.

One night, I was in the house playing my video game and getting ready to eat dinner, when my sister came into the house. She told me that my cousins wanted to see me and she also said, "I think that car they are driving is stolen, so you better not go with them." I go out to the front of the house. I say, "Whose car is this?" One of them said, "Mine". So I look at the tags. They are thirty day tags, so I said, "Let's ride." We left. That's when they said, "Do you want to get one?" I said,

"Yeah, I do." Then they told me how they broke in the car sales lot, stole all the keys, and got the cars they wanted. That night, we stole thirteen cars and had them everywhere, most of them by my house. We raced all night. I even went to pick up my brother. I'm riding without any license plates on the back. He didn't know. He thought the car was mine. But before daylight broke, we took him back to his house in a different car. I never went back home that night. So my Mom didn't know where I was at. We were at her sister's house right down the street that morning before we went to sleep. I had a feeling that the police was coming. I said, "What if the police will be knocking at the door this morning?" They told me not to say that.

Soon, before sunrise, the police came and my mother was with them. We didn't answer the door so they wouldn't think we were home. I could hear my Mom say, "I know they are in there", but they left. I felt betrayed by my mother. Now I was running; police was in that area all day long. So my cousin got us a ride, and we went to my other cousin's house. They had a barn with cable TV in it. So I stayed in there until night. Also, I called my Mom and lied. I told her I got a bus ticket to New York and hung up, because she was blowing me out. I called my sister's cell phone and told her I was alright and that I wasn't going anywhere. She told me that Mama had been crying because she doesn't want anything to happen to me. She said the police had been around my house all day and just left, so I told her that I was on my way to get some clothes. She told me to hurry up and be careful. I met my brother in the projects and told him that I'm going to stay with him for a while at my aunt's house who took custody of me. When I got to my Mom's house, I hurried and got my clothes and left to go to my aunt's. When I got to my aunt's house, she told me that my mother had been calling and that I need to call her back. I called. She told me the police said they just want to ask me some questions. I told her that I don't know anything and that they need to leave me alone. She said, "Be careful", and "Bye." That night, we rode around smoking and drinking and went back over to my aunt's house where we stayed. My aunt had to work that morning, so she left at 6:00 AM, but before she went out, she asked whether we got anything on us. We said no, and she went to work and we went back to sleep until the phone rang. It was my brother's girlfriend telling us to come to her house.

Then the phone rang again. It was my Mom. She said that we might need to leave because she thinks the police is coming. I said, "yeah, alright, they don't know where we are at unless somebody told them so". I hung up, told my brother, and started watching a DVD. Soon the movie was getting good. I heard a knock at the front door and at the garage door. I peeked out the window. It was nothing but police out there. I was going to run, but I didn't. I woke my brother up. He went to the door. They said they needed to question us, so they hand cuffed us and took me and my brother downtown, took our finger prints and locked us up for stealing thirteen cars. I was miserable.

My bound was fifty thousand dollars. I stayed in there for five days until I bonded out. It felt like I was locked up a long time. The charges got dismissed. That was my wake-up call. I started working doing concrete every day and getting paid every Friday, still smoking weed and drinking. Then one day, my brother came to me saying that he knew an easy way to make some money. He said, "How about robbing restaurants?" So that's what we started doing almost twice every week. We would go buy clothes, shoes, pay bills, and go to clubs throwing money in the air. We were having a good time. Not too long after that, in February 2006, I found out I had a baby on the way. So I chilled out, moved in with my baby's mother, continued working hard, overtime and all. Also, I bought a safe and started saving money for our baby. Once again, we started robbing. Me, I was doing it because I wanted more money than I was making working, plus I was helping pay bills and stuff, still clubbing, hanging out late. I never told my baby's mother what was going on.

Then one day, I went to my mother's house. She told me, "Whatever you are doing, you better quit." I didn't pay it any attention, though my Daddy's brother told me the same thing. I kept on doing it. Not too long after that, our baby was born on October 23, 2006. That was the happiest day of my life. She looked just like me. I stayed in the hospital with them the whole time except for when I had to wash up. That same day, I wanted to go with my brother. They were going to do another robbery, but he told me no. So I got high and drunk with him and went back to the hospital. We took the baby home, got her stuff together. Still, I went back to running the streets, doing the same as before. I was hard-headed, didn't want to listen to what people were telling me. My baby's mother and I got into an argument -- a big one. So I packed up all my things, went to my mother's house, and told her it was over. I felt bad. I went to the club that night, got drunk and went back to my Mom's house.

The next day, I went to work, got off, helped build a dog house until I got tired, and went to visit my daughter. I held her all day until I was about to call my mother to come get me, but my baby's mother asked that we start over and get back together. I did move back, but I was still running the streets. We did another robbery that week, then went and got drunk. We went to the club, where my cousin and I got into an argument and then got into a fight. I was so mad, I wanted to kill him, but I told my brother to take me home.

When I got there, my baby and her mother were asleep. All I could think about was getting my cousin the next day. I told my baby's mother about it. She told me that I need to call him, because we don't need to be fighting. So I listened to her and called him. He and my brother were about to rob another restaurant. They asked me, "Do I want to come and drive for them?" I said, "Okay." When they got to our house, the last thing I told my baby's mother was that I'll be back. Then we left the house, went to another county, and robbed the restaurant. As we were coming out of the place, the police was pulling up, so we got in the car. I started it up and pulled off as if nothing had happened. As I looked out the rearview mirror, I see the police car coming behind us fast. When I got to the stop sign, the police turned the blue lights on us. I pulled over. That's when I heard the police say, "I think these are the suspects that just robbed the store." So I punched the gas and took them on a high speed chase.

At the time, all I was thinking about was our daughter and that I should have stayed home. The chase lasted for about thirty minutes until I got on a dirt road, hit the brakes, and hit a tree at fifty miles an hour. We all jumped out and ran. I got caught first by the K-9 dog, then my baby's mother's brother, my cousin, then my brother. My bond was set at two hundred and ten thousand dollars. I knew that I wasn't going anywhere. They charged me with eight common law robberies, flee to elude arrest, possession of cocaine and marijuana -- the maximum. I was looking at three hundred and twenty four months and twenty days. I signed a plea for forty eight to sixty months. I went to prison two months later. After that I was fighting, always stressed out.

I was like that until I got here to Alexander and met my Brother Sundance. He taught me about walking the wheel. Since I joined the circle, I have been at peace. I would like to thank my Brothers Sundance, Horseshoe and Thunder for teaching me the right things about walking the Red Road. I love you all, Brothers. We are one, the Brothers of the Buffalo.

VISIONS

Walter M. Harris

As the sun rises in the morning and sets at night,
I continue an ancient and traditional rite.
For I'm a Wolf who has visions with clear sight, but as
I blink my eyes I'm an Eagle in flight, watching over my
people as they smoke their prayer pipes.
There is a sparkle in my eyes as the Raven Flies High.
A Red Horse runs until it loses a shoe.

I hear Thunder in the distance
But the sky is still blue.
I hear a Wolf that howls after dark as it prowls.
What have I become, and what must I be to keep my
people traditional and forever free?
For as the Buffalo roams this is forever our home.

So now as the sun sets, I cast my fishing net.
As I sit on a river bank, I realize
I should have made the pilgrims' ship sink,
For there has been no thanks or giving as they destroyed
my people's living
For there is a Flame that burns, and a sacred wheel we
walk.

But my eyes are open and I've finally learned.
This is the story of a Horse that is Red and a Raven that
Flies
While the Wolf leads the pack that holds all ties
While the breeze blows, the river flows for these.

Native People will never go.
Aho.

THE BOY WHO BECAME THUNDER WOLF

Thunder Wolf

I was born March 10, 1976 in Scotland County N.C. at the old hospital to the parents of "Father", the Late Great George E. L., and "Mother", Julie Ann. Up until I was about six, my father was a grave digger. We traveled around a lot until he was hurt and couldn't work no more. My mother didn't want to live in Robeson County, so we settled down in Laurinburg, North Carolina. My father's side of the family is Tuscarora, my mother's side Tuscarora and Siouan. I have an older brother and two older sisters. My brother Kenny was always my hero coming up. My sisters are Patty Gail, who is my rock, my other sister Mary, who is hard headed like I used to be, but I do love her. By age, I am the oldest of my mother and father's children, three boys.

Coming up, my father raised us to be tough and to always respect our elders. After he was hurt, he started raising hogs. We got a lot of our food from the pigs and gardens he always had. So coming up, we knew how to put food on the table. We lived in Scotland County until I was thirteen years old.

My mother ran off and left us. I was twelve, my brother John was nine, my little brother BJ was six. A lot of the cooking and cleaning was put in my hands to make sure my brothers were looked after. My Dad always made a way for us to have something to eat. Things were real hard on Dad being sick and trying to raise three boys. I used to watch him go without eating just to make sure we had enough to eat. So I started doing the same just so he would eat. I got two meals a day at school. Before Mom left, I used to love to go where every Mom wants her son to be. You could say, I was a Momma's boy. So after she left, it was really hard on me. On top of it, people were saying that my Mom didn't love or care about me. That really hurt. So I built a lot of hate in my heart toward my mother. I always would say, if my own mother didn't love me, how could I trust another woman with loving me? After she left, I would write to different states asking the police whether they could help find my mother. Time went by, then one day I went to check the mail, and there was a letter from her. We all cried, even Dad. Dad really loved Mom a lot.

She told us in the letter that she was OK. That's about it, and that she loved us. But at that time, the hate was already in my heart for her. Dad did the best he could for us boys. My Dad was a big man before he had the first stroke. Six foot three inches, three hundred pounds. Wasn't none of it fat either. But he overcame it all. My Dad's side of the family was always there for us. My Grandparents John K and Lizzie were our heart and soul. They had a big family, six boys and three girls. We loved to go stay with our grandparents and uncles and aunts. They tried to give us the love we weren't getting from our mother. My mother's father and mother and my mother's grandmother were also there for us. I had the greatest grandparents in the world on both sides of the family. My Dad's brothers were always my role models. I love them so much. Throughout life, I've learned much from them.

After Mom left, our house burned down and we lost everything we had. We had to move in with my cousin Judy Ann and her family for a few weeks until Dad got his check and rented a house in town. A couple of Indian kids in a place where we felt out of place. It was already bad enough that we had to go to school in Scotland County. We always hated it, but we were children and we didn't have any say. I used to walk about a mile and a half just to catch the bus so I wouldn't have to change schools. A lady named Mrs. Smith was the bus driver, and she broke the rules just to do this for me. She was a real sweet lady. So for about three months I did this, get up at 4:30 am every morning. Until my Dad said it was time for me to change schools.

The school I was going to had a few Indians attending. Now this new school had about eight. Most of the kids were black and about a third were white. So I finished out my seventh grade year at I. Ellis Johnson School.

During that year, someone shot into our house and hit my baby brother in the leg. So it was a crazy place we lived in. That summer we got the best news we could get. We were moving back to Robeson County. We were really happy. My great uncle Ben was a share cropper and he was retiring. He told my Dad that he could get him the house if my Dad would keep an eye on the farm for Mr. LaRue. So we moved that summer and by the time school got started back, we had a lot of Indian friends. We always had to fight in Scotland County. We just didn't fit in. If it wasn't for someone picking on our clothes, someone would pick on our long hair, or the color of our skin. So it was really great being around our own people who didn't look down on us. My mother's Mom, Ms. Jessie, came and lived with us that year to help Dad look after us. That was a good year in our life. We'd go fishing and swimming in the Lumber River in the summer. Ride our ponies and hunt in the fall, winter, and spring. My Dad and uncles taught us how to hunt and fish at an early age in life. We never wanted toys and games when we were growing up. Give us a pony, a fishing pole, or a gun and we were as happy as can be. My brothers and I were always together riding our ponies or being in the woods. But it came to an end too quickly. The farm we lived on in Maxton, off Highway 71, grew a lot of tobacco and cotton. Mr. LaRue told my Dad that he had some Mexicans coming in to work the farm for him. So he gave us thirty days to find someplace else to live. We were really sad that we had to leave all of our friends and go back to Scotland County again. We moved into one of my Dad's friends' places for a little while until we could find some place bigger. It was a two bedroom trailer. It was really small. We lived there for a couple of months. My Dad found a bigger place for us to stay. We didn't like it, but we didn't have a choice.

My Dad only got a check once every month. So he'd do what he had to do. He'd rake pine straw and we would help. And he'd put his liquor steel down and make some moon shine and grow a little pot on the side also. He was a man who did what he had to do to take care of his family the best way he could. When he moved to the new place, there was an Indian family who lived beside us. Well, the lady was half Indian, half white. The man was Indian. So we became fast friends, their family and ours. Mary and Greg were good people. They loved to party. Mary introduced my Dad to her Mom. They started talking.

Ms Mildred was a good woman. She treated my brothers and me just as we were her own children. Ms. Mildred and Dad got really close. My brothers and I wanted them to get married, but they never did. Ms. Mildred had three boys and five girls. Her husband had died of cancer. As our family got closer, our love for one another grew. As our family got bigger now, I had six brothers instead of three and seven sisters instead of two. And a woman who gave me the love my mother wasn't there to give me. So I'll always be thankful to her. My Dad kept his own house and she kept hers. About all her children were grown. So we spent a lot of time together as a family. I loved being around them, but I just didn't like living in Scotland County and going to school there. So when school started back, Mrs. Mildred's son Buck and I would skip school a lot until my Dad caught us one day hiding in the house. So I had to come up with a new plan. I started tearing my shoes up to keep from having to go. Dad couldn't afford to buy us Nikes and Reeboks. So we wore what he got us and that was that.

I had two teachers while I was in the ninth grade who were Indian: a Mrs. C. and a Mrs. L.. Mrs. L. taught Indian Ed. Mrs. C. was a counselor. They tried to keep me in school. They would come to the house and check on me. Once they even bought me some shoes. They were really some great people. I think they were the only two Indian women who worked at that school. I think that was one of the reasons they work hard so hard to help me. They wanted to see me make something of my life. So things were back to the drawing board.

Then the lady we were renting from was selling the place where we lived and where Mrs. Mildred lived. But she had a trailer park. Moving all over again, and never liked living around a lot of people. Still don't to this day. But at least were it was at, there was good hunting and some swamps we could run around in. I've smoked pot since I was real young. My mother's sister and my older cousin were the people I spent the most time with. So they would get me high. And I would steal my Dad's plants that he would grow. My brother John, Buck, and I were always into something. We were either hunting, getting high, or fighting chickens and dogs. Just being wild teenagers.

One night my life changed completely. We were at my Dad's house. He was at my uncle's house helping to kill some hogs. So it was me, John, Buck, and my little brother B.J. We all started playing around acting crazy with a gun. My brother John got the shotgun and pointed it at me and I ran. As we were watching TV, I got the gun. I thought it was on safety, but the gun went off and my brother John died in my arms. Before he died, he told me he forgave me. This is a hard part for me to talk about. See, it's something I live with every day. Just making one stupid mistake caused me to lose my best friend, my brother. What should have changed my life only made me worse. I wanted to die.

The courts charged me with manslaughter. I was taken to Raleigh. They let me go to my brother's burial. After the wake, I went back to Raleigh for a couple of months. Then I was sent to Fay Hill, NC. I was going back and forth to court. My father, my grandparents on both sides of the family were there, also my uncle Walter, my Aunt Effie from my Dad's side of the family, my mother, my uncle LC, my cousin Lisa from my Mom's side. I was lost, praying and asking God to take my life. I didn't want to live no more.

A lot of my family turned their backs on me. The court system didn't want me to go back and live with my father. My mother's father wanted me to come live with him. My Dad's brother, Uncle Walter, wanted me to live with him. My Dad's parents, my Grandmother Lizzie and Grandfather John K, wanted me to come live in Robeson County with them. They figured that it would be better for me. I love my other grandfather and my uncle, but they lived in Scotland County, and I didn't want to have to go to school there. But they were always there for me. So the court system gave me probation and I had to see a doctor at Mental Health every week. They had me doped up where all I wanted to do was sleep. They thought that it would be a good idea to let me stay out of school the rest of the year and start the next year with a fresh start.

Grandmother Lizzie and Grandfather John K: Poppa and Momma, that's what I always called them. They were so great. Poppa and I would go riding around in his car a lot. I always loved to go riding with him. Momma was really protective of us all. They were big on Church, don't miss no Church ever. So I would go with them. I mainly went because Momma wanted me to go. I loved being with my grandparents. They also had my little cousin whom they raised since he was a tiny baby. Then on the weekend, my Uncle Albert would come. I loved my Uncle Albert. He was a good dude. He taught me a lot about fishing and trapping. He was fun to talk to. Living with my grandparents, I got to be around a lot of my cousins. They never threw anything up in my face. They would always take up for me. Most of the time, my cousins Jeff, Lee, Ricky, Stevie, Kenny, and I were together. We boys spent a lot of time together. They weren't about getting into trouble. Things were going good, going to Church with my grandparents. But I still had the pain in my heart.

There was a girl at the Church whom I liked and she liked me. We knew one another our whole life. She was a true friend if there ever was one. Well, we started getting close. We would call one another and talk all the time. My grandparents liked her a lot. This went on for a couple of months. Her name was Alison Nicole. She was so sweet. One night she called me and we talked for a while. She told me that she would call me Friday night when she got back from her grandparents' house. But the phone call I got wasn't the one I wanted. I was at the pond behind our house and my grandmother called me to the house. But as I was fishing, I kept hearing a boy and girl talking, but I never saw anybody.

As my grandmother called me again, I knew something was wrong. As I saw the tears on her face, I was really scared. My grandmother was a strong woman. She reached out for me and hugged me. She told me that Alison and her brother Tony got killed in a car wreck. I couldn't take it no more. I held up to after their wake. I was done with Church. God didn't care for me. He took away everyone who ever cared for me.

I started eating pills real bad, smoking reefer. I was stoned all the time. I started selling cocaine at the age of fifteen, running around with my other cousins, who, as they say, were the black sheep of the family. I fitted right into the crew. I kept it away from my grandparents until I turned sixteen and got my license. My father got me a truck. I stayed at the dope houses, getting money, running with the fast life. Coming in late, not going to school, doing what I wanted to do. I had gotten me a 38 and I would keep it and my drugs in the barn behind my grandparents' house. Granny found it one day and told me that if that's the lifestyle I wanted to live, I had to leave. It hurt me to see her cry. But I was hooked to the life. Where we live, they call it Jonesville and it goes down there better known as "Little Miami."
So I moved in with my cousin. We pumped cocaine and reefer twenty-four seven. We were fighting chicken and pitts, selling drugs. We made a lot of money, my cousin and I. But all good things come to an end. We got busted one night. We were sitting outside beside the fire, drinking some beer and eating some pain pills. And the cops ran up on us. I guess I was lucky that night. I only had some reefer on me. My cousin had sixteen grams of cocaine. So we both went to jail. We were there for three weeks before we got out. My cousin told me he

was done with the drug game. So we parted ways. He went to work.

I went to my Dad's house. At this time, he and Ms. Mildred were living together. I would help my Dad and Buck rake pine straw. Buck was like a brother to me. So we'd smoke reefer and fight chicken when we weren't working. I lived there with them for about six months and then I was gone again. I moved to Wagram, NC, up in the Sandhills. It was OK. I was selling cocaine, making a little money, so it was OK as long as the money came in. But I was young and dumb. I bought a lot of stolen stuff and the dude I got it from got locked up. And he told them I had the stuff and that I was with him. So I ran, went down to Hoke County with some of my homeboys. I hid my truck and started hanging sheetrock with them. So after about four months, someone told the cops were I was and early one Saturday morning, they rolled up and got me. So off to Laurinburg Jail I went.

I called my Dad and told him to get my truck. I was just seventeen years old, locked up for something I didn't do, and charged with six counts of breaking and entering. I stayed in jail two weeks until they dropped my bond to five thousand dollars. My uncle Walter came and got me out. So I was back to Dad's again. One day I was at the store and I met a dude named Tommy Lee who worked in vinyl. He asked me if I wanted a job. So I took it. The dude was wild as hell so we got real tight. Not only were we working, we also started selling cocaine. We'd go to the club every weekend and fight, do all kind of crazy stuff. We had a crew. About seven of us were always together. One of my homeys was a gang banger, so we all got put down. And we cared it hard. "Want some, get some" -- that was the way we got down. Time was going by. My lawyer kept getting my case put off. I finally had to go to court. I had just turned eighteen. I went in front of the judge and he gave me eight years CYO (Committed Youthful Offender). Off to prison I went to the High Rise. When I got off the bus, I didn't know what to think. There were about sixteen of us getting off the bus. They stripped us of all our clothes. Made us put on the prison browns. As we were going to the floors where we would be housed on, the first thing we saw was a dude with a fork sticking in the side of his neck. I knew it was on then. I hadn't let anybody known I was going to get time. So nobody knew where I was at but my homey TJ and my girlfriend Tracey. She told my Dad were I was at.

After about two months I was there, I get a letter from my Dad. He was hurt that I hadn't let him know where I was at. I wrote him and told him that I was tired of putting him through so much. I just wanted to do this by myself. He wrote me back and told me if I needed him to just write. So here I'm working on an eight year bid. My homeys and my girl are riding it out with me. I'm going to get it hard, fighting, doing what I have to, to get a name for myself. Then one day I get a letter from my girlfriend's sister for me to call. So I call and get the news that my girlfriend is cheating on me just after two months. So now I'm really mad. And she is trying to lie to me about it. Then my programmer calls me to her office and tells me I got honor grade and I'll be shipping out to Sand Hills in Hoke County.

When I get there, I call my father and let him know that I am closer to home. So he came and saw me. I told him that my programmer had asked me for a home plan, could I give them his address. So three weeks later, I was back on the streets. Ninety days off eight years couldn't tell me anything. My Dad had gotten me a white and blue Z28 Camaro. By the time the probation officer had dropped me off, I was gone again, looking for my homeys so we could party. And party we did. I even checked my old girlfriend out just for the sex and to do her like she done me. I went back to work with my homey Tommy Lee and hooked up with these two girls. One was older and lived in Red Springs, the other one was younger than me. Tommy and I moved to Laurel Hill N.C. I started right back selling cocaine. I left the two girls alone and hooked up with Tonya, who later would have my three girls. We talked for a while, and then broke up. I met Carrie, who was one bad chick I had to have. At first it wasn't love, it was lust. She schooled me to the game. So she gets pregnant with our child. My homey and I fell out. I was nineteen years old with a woman telling me she's going to have my baby. I was scared to death, so we started fussing all the time. I still had all this hate in my heart about my mother. If I couldn't trust her with loving me, then how could I believe what Carrie was telling me? So I burn out on her. My father finds out and rents a house for her to live in with him. He was real happy about being a grand daddy and getting to spend time with his grandchild.

By now I am hooked on the pain pills real bad. I'm living in a trailer park in Laurinburg, still selling crack cocaine, hiding from Carrie and my probation officer. He wants to lock me up. She wants to fuss and raise sand. Once again, someone tells the cops where I'm at and my sorry cousin Lisa lets them in on me. I think she did it just so she and her crack head boyfriend could get my stash. Off again to prison, this time to the old Polk where it was really rough. I stayed there about six months. Carrie and I got back together, and I went back to Sand Hills. And she would come see me every week with my father. On Feb. 2, 1996, she gave birth to our little girl Shian Deon. I was so happy when I got to see my baby girl and hold her in my arms.

While I was in prison, I had a courier who would bring me drugs. My father would drop them off beside the fence and when I would go to work at the school, I'd pick up the trash and I'd get it. I'd sneak money out to him on visits when he'd come see me. They put me in segregation for selling drugs in prison. Altogether, I stayed in prison about two years. A couple of weeks before I got out, my Dad and Carrie came to see me. And I had already heard that she had been seeing some dude. After the visit, she leaves town with my little girl and goes to Ohio. Now I was really mad.

So I finally come home to my Dad's. I go get me a new ride. Buy me some more chicken and dogs. On top of some more cocaine. I am right back to the same old thing and running around with all kinds of women. One day I see Tonya at the store, and she has a little girl about two years old. Tonya's mother says she's mine. So we get back together and she moves in with me. Then Carrie brings Shian down for a couple of weeks, and I have Lisa and Shian together.

If Lisa "Pooh" is not mine by blood, she is mine by heart. And I love her just the same. I really tried to give Tonya my heart. She got pregnant with Raven. Then I found out that she cheated on me. The trust was broken after Raven was born. We had a blood test. It came back ninety-nine point nine percent to the Native American race. She was mine. I tried to make it work for my girls. I didn't want them to come up like I did. But if there was no trust and love, it wouldn't work. So we fuss and fight all the time. She'd get me locked up for stupid stuff. I would try to go on with my life, but she just wouldn't let me. So I end back in prison for one hundred and twenty days. When I get out, I finally go back to Jonesville in Maxton, my hometown. By now my grandparents have passed on to the next life in the great beyond.

I'm loving it that living in Jonesville ain't got the drama. Then Tonya finds out that I'm out and she comes around again. After a couple of months, she starts fussing, coming to my house, jumping on girls I'd have there, going to my friends, jumping on girls there. She wouldn't let it go. My homey Snubb was living with me at the time. Both of us were half crazy and didn't take junk from anybody. Then we got dragged into some mess with Eddie Hatcher. The SBI ran up in our spot looking for Eddie. After they got Eddie somewhere else, they still kept bothering us. So we went our own way. My Godfather Robert took me to meet this dude down the road that I knew of, but had never dealt with. He loved them chicken and I did, too. So we became fast friends, a friendship that formed like brothers. He was a mad man also. I moved in with him and we got money together for a long time.

By me and Phillip becoming the best of friends, I meet the woman who would do what no other woman could do. But I still was trying to be the father my Dad was. The love was gone, but I still tried to make it work with Tonya. She got pregnant again with Ashley. She was about five months pregnant when we both realized it wasn't going to work. I was really in love for the first time in my life. I fell in love with my best friend's sister. Amber Nicole was the woman I always dreamed about. My heart was putty in her hands. I have never felt this way about another woman. She always tried to get me to get a job. But the drug game had me. I robbed this dude who tried to play me. The dude was telling people he was going to get me, so I went looking for him. I would pull in his yard with my homeys and he would run in his house.

My Dad passed away in October 2000. I lost it for real. My Dad was my everything. He told me that he was proud of me the night before he died. After the wake, I did get strung out on pills again. I left Amber and moved to 501 with some dudes I thought were real. We made a lot of money. We got in some beef with some dudes. They shot into my homey's house and hit my man Nick. And my homeys Black Bart, Little Time, and I put pain on their whole crew. It went on for a few months. I got trapped off with some crack cocaine and had to go to prison again for eleven to fourteenth months. While I am in jail, I find out Amber's going to have a baby. I was happy and sad. I was happy because I loved her so much. I was sad because I wouldn't be there for our child's birth. Back to prison I went.

I've always known about the sacred hoop for our people. I was just into them streets with so much hate in my heart. While I was in prison, the Feds got my best friend Phillip. Amber had our little girl Nakiya. After the Feds got my friend, I came home and went back to the same old thing. A dude whom I would have given my life for at one time put me back on. "A" was my dog for years, but he's done like the rest. He turned his back on me. I've been a person who could let people, whom I thought were my friends, lead me astray.

I planned to kill a man who was the cousin of the woman I loved more than life. I walked all the way to his front door. And something just wouldn't let me go through with it. The year of 2002, I was out there. I had a death wish. I couldn't get anybody to grant it for me. Everybody who really cared for me, I pushed them away. I was running with a crew that was off the chain.

My man Snubb had beat a murder charge and we put down one of the meanest drug empires. It was to be "down or lay down." We had gotten big headed. We walk into a club and they would make a path for us. They called us the untouchables. The whole crew was gun slingers and cutters. We were making money and getting crazier and crazier by the day. We really thought we were unstoppable. At one time, I would have died for every one of the dudes from Jonesville.

March 27, 2003, I thought my death wish had come true. We were told that there were twenty kilo of cocaine, one hundred pounds of reefer, no telling how much money. My homey Little Time and I went after it. We got his two uncles to go with us. The woman lied to us. I still don't know why she did what she did, but things didn't go as planned and a man lost his life for nothing. For about eight months, they were talking about the death penalty. I thought I was going to get my wish. But I didn't want anybody to put a needle in me. I wanted to go out with a blaze of glory with my MAC 90 in my hands. So after they dropped the death penalty, my lawyer and PI came to see me, Mr. Trenkle and Ms Etta. Not only were they my lawyer and PI, they are now my family and two of my best friends in the world whom I love dearly. Well, they came with a plea for thirty-five years. I turned it down. Mr. Trenkle finally got a plea for twenty-one years eleven months to twenty six years eleven months, so I took it. I didn't want to die no more. I realized what the Creator wanted me to do. I realized what I was throwing away. My children. My family. The only woman I ever loved. I let them all down.

It took years for me to let all the hate go out of my heart. I had to forgive myself before I could forgive anybody else. When I forgave my mother, it felt like the world came off my back. When I went to Court, Amber, Uncle Jason, Aunts Effie, Lorie, Cousins Lizzie, Alice, Ciarra were there plus Raven and Ashley. Aunt Katy was there for me. All the hard core left me. I cried. They sent me to Central Prison to get started on my time. They didn't have a prayer circle there. I stayed there for three weeks and then they sent me to Elizabeth City, "The Tank." The prayer circle was crazy there. An old Indian man named David Dollar let me smoke his pipe and I asked the Creator to show me what he wanted me to do. So I fasted and prayed and he sent the White Buffalo to show me the way. You don't ever tell your whole vision. So that's all I'll tell of mine.

The Creator showed me what he wanted me to do. Teach his children, show them the Red Road and how to walk the way of our ancestors. I went from a person who didn't care if he lived or died to a man who has so much love to give the world. The hardest thing for me was to put everything in the Creator's care. Being in here with the time I got is the hardest. I've lost so many loved ones. My Grandfather Leo, Uncles Thomas, Curtis, and Albert, and Aunt Jean, Friends Chad and so many others whom I loved dearly. But I know they are in a better place. Doesn't anything happen unless he wants it to happen. I don't have but about three true friends, and my family. My mother still won't write me. But I ask the Creator to be with her and keep her safe. Walking in the way of my ancestors has helped me so much in my life. I used to be a person who didn't care about living, much less anything else. Got hooked on pain pills to kill the pain I kept hidden inside. I'd eat pills from sun up to sun down. I was too stupid to see that not only was I killing myself, I also was killing the ones who loved me. I thought the world was against me. Now I realize I was the only one against me. I always tried to do what everybody else wanted me to do. Some of my family would try to push Church on me. I don't have anything against Church, but I feel every man has to walk his own path in life. But I did try Church, because my family wanted me to. I just couldn't find the peace I was looking for.

My sacred pipe is my bible. Now I feel I'm walking the right path in life, teaching my brothers and sisters about our ancestors and our way of life. Now my eyes are open to see the beauty, balance and harmony of creation. I always try to walk in the way of my ancestors. It's up to us to teach the next generation. I'll be the first to say I don't know everything, but I'm learning as I journey through life. The brothers and sisters I meet along the way are a big help. We learn from one another. Also, I read, and most of all, I learn from Mother Earth, Father Sky and all my relations. There's no better teacher.

You have to become one with your relations. I feel now that I'm the man my Father and my Grandparents would be proud of. I had to give everyone and everything I love away to find my true path in life. My family and my true friends have been a blessing to me. I was twenty-seven old when I came to prison. I wasted most of them twenty-seven years. I've been in here going on eight years. I have fourteen years six months left. Some would say I've wasted these twenty-one years eleven months. But if you've walked a mile in my shoes, you would see the difference. I went from a kid praying for death every day to a drug dealer, gang banger, "kill or be killed" kind of person. My life was a train running out of control, waiting on that wreck to take me out. I am thankful in life now that I didn't get killed and I pray for the man's life that I took. I hope his family can one day find it in their hearts to forgive me for what I've done. My heart is full of love now, no more hurt and pain. I don't need the drugs anymore to kill and hide the pain. I have the Creator and my family.

To hear my family and the ones I love tell me they are proud of the person I've become: that's what's up. Prison can't change who you are. You have to want to change. And I'm tired of the life I lived. I don't want people to talk about the person I was when my time does come. I want them to talk about the good I have done for my people. It's time to help our people and stop hurting them. Travel your own road in life, trust in the Creator. You'll never go wrong.

To my family who have stuck by me and gave me the support that I truly needed, Uncles Jason, Walter, Lee, John, LC, Sam and Jordan, Aunts Effie, Laurie, Booties, Frances, Doris, Lizzie, Susie, and Cierra. To my children Elisa, ShIan, Raven, Nacoma, and Nakiya. To the three wonder women who always gave me the love of a mother, Daffine Talley, Mildred Dimery, and Effie Lowery. My sister Patty Gail, I love you, baby. Last but not least to the one person who has been there from day one, Amber Nicole, my heart will always belong to you and thank you for always being a true friend. You all are the reason I've become the person I am today. My Grandmother Jessie, I love you always. For the ones who already passed over, I hope I've finally become the man you said I would be one day. There is a place behind the moon. Please wait for me there.

I pray that by you reading about some parts of my life, it'll help you take the right path in life. Go to school, make good grades, listen to your parents and elders. They know what they are talking about. Always put family first, they'll be there when all else falls short. Most of all, keep your faith in the Creator. He took the weight off my past. To my birth mother Julie, I've forgiven you a long time ago. Now it's time to forgive yourself. To all my brothers and sisters behind these stonewalls, stay strong. To Chief Leon Locklear, Medicine Wolf, Grandmother War Eagle, White Wolf, thanks for coming into my life. The Red Road has saved my life. I pray that you, the reader, do not still think that drugs and money are all good. Being in prison and losing everyone you love – no amount of money can replace that.

To my beautiful children Elisa, Shian, Raven, Nacoma, and Nakiya: I hope and pray that you don't hate me. I've made mistakes in life I'm paying for. And I can

be a father from behind these walls. If I can keep you all and your cousins from making the same mistakes I made in life, this time will not be wasted. To my people, the Tuscarora Nation of North Carolina, stay strong and true. I am thankful for everyone who has stuck by me: Snubb, Buffalo, West Wind. Walk proud, my Brothers. Stay Red. Aho. Just the beginning.
Taylorsville, NC 28681

THUNDER

Red Horse

Hear the Thunder, see the lightning.
I roar like a lion, parading the pride,
standing tall and true to the calling.

Hear the Thunder, see the lightning.
With every flash, with every boom
I become stronger,
standing tall and true.

ENDNOTES

Introduction

[1] Joy Harjo, "Eagle Pom" in BrIan Swann, editor, *Native American Songs and Poems. An Anthology* (Mineola, New York: Dover, 1996), 39.
[2] On stereotypes, see Devon A.Mihesuah, *American Indians. Stereotypes and Realities* (Atlanta, Georgia: Clarity International, reprint 2001).
[3] The following information can be found on the website of the North Carolina Commission of Indian Affairs at http://www.doa.state.nc.us/cia/ (accessed December 2011).
[4] In the genre of comedy, American Indian experiences of the prison system were the focus of the popular film *PowWow Highway* (Jonathan Wacks, 1988).
[5] Harvey Arden,editor, *Leonard Peltier, United States Prisoner # 88637-132. Prison Writings: My Life is My Sun Dance* (New York: St. Martin's Press, 1999).
[6] For a history of the relationship between American Indian nations and the United States as it relates to the prison system, see Luana Ross, *Inventing the Savage. The Social Construction of Native American Criminality* (Austin, Texas: University of Texas Press, 1998), 9-73. Walter Echo-Hawk, *Study of Native American Prisoner Issues* (Boulder, Colorado: Native American Rights Fund, 1996).
[7] Ross, 14. For a successful contemporary implementation, see MarIanne O. Nielsen and James W. Zion, *Navajo Nation Peacemaking: Living Traditional Justice* (Tucson: University of Arizona, 2005), and The Honorable Robert Yazzie, Chief Justice of the Navajo Nation, "Navajo Justice" in *Yes! A Journal of Positive Futures* (Fall 2000), 36-38. In the words of the Chief Justice, "In Navajo peacemaking, offenders are brought in to a session involving the person accused of an offense

and the person who suffered from it, along with the 'tag-along' victims of the crime, namely the relatives of the accused and of the person hurt by the accused...The sessions are moderated by a community leader called a 'peacemaker'. The action is put on the table. People talk about what happened and how they feel about it...Traditional Navajo law requires families to take responsibility for their family members." "Navajo Justice", 36-37. See also the Indigenous Peacemaking Initiative at the Native American Rights Fund at http://www.narf.org/cases/manypaths.html.

[8] To quote the homepage of the Robert Sundance Family Wellness Center, "The Robert Sundance story demonstrates that one man, notably one from the fringes of society, can change 'the system.' Robert was an American Indian from the Standing Rock Reservation in South Dakota who was introduced to alcohol at an early age. After spending nearly twenty-five years on skid rows across the American west, drunk, homeless, stricken over 250 times with DTs (Delirium Tremens), and illegally arrested nearly 500 times, Sundance decided to reform the system that unjustifiably incarcerated homeless street alcoholics. Alcohol killed most of his drinking friends and counterparts, and it certainly could have killed him. His eventual "Sundance Court Case" led to radical reform of the process of arrest and conviction of public inebriates, and it helped create the process of alcoholic rehabilitation. No other single individual had done more to improve the American system of justice in regard to public Alcoholism." http://www.uaii.org/ (accessed December 2011).

[9] For a case study, see Elizabeth S. Grobsmith, *Indians in Prison. Incarcerated Native Americans in Nebraska* (Lincoln and London: University of Nebraska Press, 1994). The author concludes her award-winning study by noting that "it would be a fair characterization to say that for Nebraska inmates, every single cultural or religious

freedom gained for prisoners represents an outcome of a battle. Indian people have become accustomed to having to draw major attention to their concerns before they are able to obtain relief; it will be no different for Indian prisoners" (Grobsmith, 176). For a recent example of successful collaboration between a native non-profit organization and state prisons, see "United Indians to Provide Religious Services to Native Inmates in Washington Prisons", http://www.americanIndianreport.com/wordpress/2011/06/united-Indians-to-provide-religious-services-to-native-inmates-in-washington-prisons/ (accessed December 2011).

[10]http://www.aclu.org/aclu-defense-religious-practice-and-expression (accessed December 2011).

[11] James B. Waldram, *The Way of the Pipe. Aboriginal Spirituality and Symbolic Healing in CanadIan Prisons* (Toronto: Broadview Press, 1997).

[12] http://www.historicaltrauma.com; for a bibliography of Maria Yellow Horse Braveheart's research, see http://www.columbia.edu/cu/ssw/faculty/profiles/braveheart.html (accessed December 2011).

[13] Chief Justice Robert Yazzie, op.cit., 37.

[14] All statistical information as collected by BJS, is found at http://bjs.ojp.usdoj.gov/content/pub/pdf/p10.pdf (accessed December 2011).

[15] Governor's Crime Commission, North Carolina Criminal Justice Analysis Center, *System Stats* (Summer 1999), Introduction.

[16] The Tribal Court Clearing House project offers in-depth information on tribal court systems at http://www.tribal-institute.org/lists/justice.htm (accessed December 2011).

[17] See Eva Mary Garroutte, *Real Indians: Identity and the Survival of Native America* (Berkeley: University of California Press, 2003); MaximilIan C. Forte, editor, *Indigenous Resurgence in the Caribbean. AmerIndian*

Survival and Revival (New York: Peter Lang, 2006); Kurly Tlapoyawa, *We Will Rise. Rebuilding the Mexikah Nation* (Victoria, B.C.: Trafford, 2000), William Loren Katz, *Black Indians. A Hidden Heritage* (New York: Simon and Schuster, 1997); Gabrielle Tayac, "IndiVisible: Family Histories and the Making of an Exhibition at the National Museum of the American Indian" in Anthony Parent and Ulrike Wiethaus, editors, *Trauma and Resilience in American Indian and African American Southern History* (New York: Peter Lang, forthcoming).

[18] See Vine Deloria, Jr., and Clifford M. Lytle, *The Nations Within. The Past and Future of American Indian Sovereignty* (Austin: University of Texas Press, 1984); David E. Wilkins and Heidi Kiiwetinepinesiik Stark, *American Indian Politics and the American Political System* (Lanham, Maryland: Rowman and Littlefield, 3rd edition, 2010).

[19] See Laura F. Klein and LillIan A. Ackerman, editors, *Women and Power in Native North America* (Norman and London: University of Oklahoma Press, 1995); on American Indian women inmates and US incarceration, see Ross, op.cit.

[20] See U.S. Census Bureau, *We the People: American Indians and Alaska Natives in the United States,* http://www.census.gov/prod/2006pubs/censr-28.pdf (issued in 2006).

[21] See Charles C. Mann, *1491. New Revelations of the Americas before Columbus* (New York: Alfred Knopf, 2005).

[22] Ross, op.cit., 93.

Two Crow Feathers, *Thank the Creator for Today*

[23] See Taylor, Nathaniel G., et al., (1910) *Papers Relating to Talks and Councils Held with the Indians in*

Dakota and Montana in the years 1866-1869. Washington: Government Printing Office. (Original in the National Archives, Records of the Indian Division, Office of the Secretary of the Interior, Record Group 48.)

Snow Hawk, *More than One Way of Seeing*

[24]Source: Richard Erdoes and Alfonso Ortíz, *American Indian Myths and Legends* (New York: Pantheon Publisher, 1985).
[25] As collected by Evan T. Pritchard in *Native American Stories of the Sacred* (Woodstock, Vermont: Sky Light Path Publishing, 2005).
[26] From Richard Erdoes and John Fire Lame Deer, *Lame Deer: Seeker of Visions* (New York: Doubleday, revised edition, 1994).

[27] Something I want to share here is a little piece of information I learned from a good friend, brother, and teacher who grew up on the Pine Ridge Reservation and the Red Cloud Reservation. He is Lakota and it drives him crazy to hear to the word Mitakuye Oyasin, "All my relations", pronounced wrong, so as a small token of my respect and appreciation for his guidance, it is pronounced Me-tauk-oo-ye O-yash-ing.

BROTHERS OF THE BUFFALO PRAYER CIRCLE
ALEXANDER CORRECTIONAL INSTITUITON
TAYLORSVILLE, NC, 2011